30 DEVOTIONS

GOD'S PLAN
for YOUR LIFE
OVERCOMING
GRIEF

BIBLICAL PRINCIPLES TO GUIDE YOU
IN YOUR JOURNEY THROUGH GRIEF

FAMILY
Christian Stores®

Scripture quotations are taken from:

The Holy Bible, King James Version (KJV)

The Holy Bible, New International Version (NIV) Copyright © 1973, 1978, 1984, by International Bible Society. Used by permission of Zondervan Publishing House. All rights reserved.

The Holy Bible, New King James Version (NKJV) Copyright © 1982 by Thomas Nelson, Inc. Used by permission.

Holy Bible, New Living Translation, (NLT) copyright © 1996. Used by permission of Tyndale House Publishers, Inc., Wheaton, Illinois 60189. All rights reserved.

The Message (MSG)- This edition issued by contractual arrangement with NavPress, a division of The Navigators, U.S.A. Originally published by NavPress in English as THE MESSAGE: The Bible in Contemporary Language copyright 2002-2003 by Eugene Peterson. All rights reserved.

New Century Version®. (NCV) Copyright © 1987, 1988, 1991 by Word Publishing, a division of Thomas Nelson, Inc. All rights reserved. Used by permission.

The New American Standard Bible®, (NASB) Copyright © 1960, 1962, 1963, 1968, 1971, 1972, 1973, 1975, 1977, 1995 by The Lockman Foundation. Used by permission.

The Holman Christian Standard Bible™ (HCSB) Copyright © 1999, 2000, 2001 by Holman Bible Publishers. Used by permission.

Cover Design & Page Layout by Bart Dawson

ISBN 978-1-58334-013-4

Printed in the United States of America

30 DEVOTIONALS

God's plan
for Your Life
Overcoming Grief

BIBLICAL PRINCIPLES TO GUIDE YOU
IN YOUR JOURNEY THROUGH GRIEF

TABLE OF CONTENTS

INTRODUCTION

*"We know that all things work together
for the good of those who love God:
those who are called according to His purpose."*

Romans 8:28 HCSB

God's Word promises that all things work together for the good of those who love Him. Yet sometimes we encounter situations that seem so troubling—or so tragic—that we simply cannot comprehend how these events might be a part of God's plan for our lives. We experience some deeply significant loss: perhaps the death of a loved one; perhaps the loss of health; perhaps divorce, job loss, or a broken personal relationship. Whatever the nature of the loss, its pain is so profound that we honestly wonder if recovery is possible. But with God, all things are possible.

The Christian faith, as communicated through the words of the Holy Bible, is a healing faith. It offers comfort in times of trouble, courage for our fears, and hope instead of hopelessness. For Christians, the grave is not a final resting place; it is a place of transition. Through the healing words of God's promises, Christians understand that the Lord continues to manifest His plan in good times and bad.

If you are experiencing the intense pain of a recent loss, or if you are still mourning a loss from long ago, this book is intended to help. So, during the next 30 days, try this experiment: read one chapter a day and take the ideas in that chapter to heart. Then, apply those lessons to the everyday realities of your life. When you weave God's message into the fabric of your day, you'll quickly discover that God's Word has the power to change everything, including you.

Grief is not meant to be avoided or feared; it is meant to be worked through. If this text assists you, even in a small way, as you move through and beyond your pain, it will have served its purpose. May God bless you and keep you, and may He place His healing hand upon your heart today and forever.

Day 1

GOD'S PLAN AND YOUR GRIEF

The Lord will work out his plans for my life—
for your faithful love, O Lord, endures forever.

Psalm 138:8 NLT

THE FOCUS FOR TODAY

Suffering may be someone's fault or it may not be
anyone's fault. But if given to God, our suffering becomes
an opportunity to experience the power of God
at work in our lives and to give glory to Him.

Anne Graham Lotz

It's an age-old riddle: Why does God allow us to endure grief? After all, since we trust that God is all-powerful, and since we trust that His hand shapes our lives, why doesn't He simply rescue us—and our loved ones—from all hardship and suffering?

God's Word teaches us again and again that He loves us and wants the best for us. And the Bible also teaches us that God is ever-present and always watchful. So why, we wonder, if God is really so concerned with every detail of our lives, does He permit us to endure emotions like grief, sadness, shame, or fear? And why does He allow tragic circumstances to invade the lives of good people? These questions perplex us, especially when our losses are staggering.

On occasion, all of us must endure life-changing personal losses that leave us breathless. When we pass through the dark valleys of life, we often ask, "Why me?" We wonder, again and again, why God allows us to suffer.

Even when we cannot understand God's plans, we must trust them. And even when we are impatient for our situations to improve, we must trust God's timing. If we seek to live in accordance with His plan for our lives, we must continue to study His Word, and we must be watchful for His signs, knowing that in time, He will lead us through the valleys, onward to the mountaintop.

FINDING NEW MEANING

Perhaps your loss has turned your world upside down. Perhaps everything in your life has been changed forever. Perhaps your relationships and your responsibilities have been permanently altered. If so, you may come face to face with the daunting task of finding a new purpose for living.

God still has an important plan for your life, and part of His plan may well be related to your grief. Your suffering carries with it great potential: the potential for intense personal growth and the potential to help others. As you begin to reorganize your life, always be watchful for ways to use your suffering for the betterment of others. Lend your experienced hand to help fellow travelers, knowing with assurance that the course of your healing will depend upon how quickly you discover new people to help and new reasons to live.

As you move through and beyond your grief, be mindful of this fact: As a wounded survivor, you will have countless opportunities to serve others. And by serving others, you will bring glory to God and meaning to the suffering you've endured.

SOMETHING TO REMEMBER

Even when you cannot understand why things happen, you must continue to trust your heavenly Father. Ruth Bell Graham once said, "When I am dealing with an all-powerful, all-knowing God, I, as a mere mortal, must offer my petitions not only with persistence, but also with patience. Someday I'll know why." So even when you can't understand why God allows certain things to happen, you must trust Him and never lose faith!

MORE FROM GOD'S WORD ABOUT GOD'S PLAN

People may make plans in their minds, but the Lord decides what they will do.

Proverbs 16:9 NCV

There is no wisdom, no insight, no plan that can succeed against the Lord.

Proverbs 21:30 NIV

Unless the Lord builds a house, the work of the builders is useless.

Psalm 127:1 NLT

MORE POWERFUL IDEAS ABOUT GOD'S PLAN

Our valleys may be filled with foes and tears, but we can lift our eyes to the hills to see God and the angels.

Billy Graham

Are you weak? Weary? Confused? Troubled? Pressured? How is your relationship with God? Is it held in its place of priority? I believe the greater the pressure, the greater your need for time alone with Him.

Kay Arthur

God knows exactly how much you can take, and He will never permit you to reach a breaking point.

Barbara Johnson

The cross that Jesus commands you and me to carry is the cross of submissive obedience to the will of God, even when His will includes suffering and hardship and things we don't want to do.

Anne Graham Lotz

In heaven, we will see that nothing, absolutely nothing, was wasted, and that every tear counted and every cry was heard.

Joni Eareckson Tada

QUESTIONS TO CONSIDER

Since I believe that God has a plan for my life, do I believe that He can help me overcome my grief?

_____

_____

Do I regularly ask God to reveal His plans to me, and when I pray, do I listen carefully for His response?

_____

_____

Do I talk to God many times each day, and am I continually asking Him to heal my heart and guide my path?

_____

_____

A PRAYER FOR TODAY

Dear Lord, even when my heart is broken,
I will earnestly seek Your will for my life. You have
a plan for me that I can never fully understand. But
You understand. And I will trust You today,
tomorrow, and forever. Amen

Day 2

IT'S POSSIBLE TO HEAL

Is anything too hard for the LORD?
Genesis 18:14 KJV

THE FOCUS FOR TODAY

The grace of God is sufficient for all our needs, for every problem and for every difficulty, for every broken heart, and for every human sorrow.

Peter Marshall

Wchen you find yourself caught in the emotional quicksand called grief, you may wonder if you'll ever recover. When the feelings of sorrow are intense, you may think—mistakenly—that the pain will never subside. But the good news is this: while time heals many wounds, God has the power to heal them all.

Ours is a God of infinite power and possibilities. But sometimes, because of limited faith and limited understanding, we wrongly assume that God cannot or will not intervene in the affairs of everyday life. Such assumptions are simply wrong.

God is busily at work in the world, and your world. Your job is to ask Him—fervently and often—for the things you need.

Have you sincerely asked God for His help as you begin the healing process? Have you asked Him to lead you on the first step back to recovery? Have you prayed for the peace that passes all understanding? If so, you're on the right track. If not, it's time to abandon your doubts and reclaim your faith in God's promises.

God's Holy Word makes it clear: absolutely nothing is impossible for Him. And since the Bible means what it says, you can be comforted in the knowledge that the Creator of the universe can do miraculous things in your own life and in the lives of your loved ones. Your challenge, as a believer, is to take God at His word, and to wait patiently for Him to bless you with peace that flows from His miraculous healing touch.

SOMETHING TO REMEMBER

God is in the business of doing miraculous things. You should form the habit of asking God for the things you need. So ask God to begin healing your heart today.

MORE FROM GOD'S WORD ABOUT GOD'S POWER

For His divine power has given us everything required for life and godliness, through the knowledge of Him who called us by His own glory and goodness.

2 Peter 1:3 HCSB

For the LORD your God is God of gods and Lord of lords, the great God, mighty and awesome.

Deuteronomy 10:17 NIV

I pray also that you will have greater understanding in your heart so you will know the hope to which he has called us and that you will know how rich and glorious are the blessings God has promised his holy people. And you will know that God's power is very great for us who believe.

Ephesians 1:18-19 NCV

With God's power working in us, God can do much, much more than anything we can ask or imagine.

Ephesians 3:20 NCV

Proclaim the power of God, whose majesty is over Israel, whose power is in the skies. You are awesome, O God, in your sanctuary; the God of Israel gives power and strength to his people. Praise be to God!

Psalm 68:34-35 NIV

MORE POWERFUL IDEAS ABOUT GOD'S POWER

God can heal the brokenhearted if all the pieces are given to Him.

Warren Wiersbe

When we face an impossible situation, all self-reliance and self-confidence must melt away; we must be totally dependent on Him for the resources.

Anne Graham Lotz

I believe that the Creator of this universe takes delight in turning the terrors and tragedies that come with living in this old, fallen domain of the devil and transforming them into something that strengthens our hope, tests our faith, and shows forth His glory.

Al Green

Whatever hallway you're in—no matter how long, how dark, or how scary—God is right there with you.

Bill Hybels

When all else is gone, God is still left. Nothing changes Him.

Hannah Whitall Smith

As sure as God puts
his children in the furnace,
he will be in the furnace
with them.

—

C. H. Spurgeon

Beware of the tendency to water down the supernatural in religion.

Oswald Chambers

Faith means believing in realities that go beyond sense and sight. It is the awareness of unseen divine realities all around you.

Joni Eareckson Tada

God's grace and power seem to reach their peak when we are at our weakest point.

Anne Graham Lotz

What we are powerless to do in our own lives, Christ was powerful enough to accomplish for everyone who would believe.

Bill Hybels

Lord, what joy to know that Your powers are so much greater than those of the enemy.

Corrie ten Boom

The impossible is exactly what God does.

Oswald Chambers

QUESTIONS TO CONSIDER

Do I place my hopes in God?

_____

_____

Despite the pain that I am feeling today, do I sincerely believe that, with God's help, I can one day find relief from my suffering?

_____

_____

Do I place limitations on myself, and do I place limitations on God's power to heal me and to use me for His purposes?

_____

_____

A PRAYER FOR TODAY

Dear Lord, absolutely nothing is impossible for You. Let me trust in Your power and in Your ability to heal me. When I lose hope, give me faith; when others lose hope, let me tell them of Your glorious works. Today, Lord, keep me mindful that You are a God of infinite possibilities and infinite love. Amen

Day 3

THE GRIEVING PROCESS

The Lord is near to those who have a broken heart.
Psalm 34:18 NKJV

THE FOCUS FOR TODAY

Grief is the aftermath of any deeply significant loss.
Wayne Oates

Grief is a uniquely personal experience. But grief is also a universal experience, a journey that has been clearly mapped by those who have documented the common elements of human suffering.

Grief usually begins with shock and then gives way to intense pain. Over time, as the mourner regains his or her emotional balance, the pain begins to fade. Gradually—sometimes almost imperceptibly—a new life is raised from the ashes of the old. And even though the mourner may never "get over" his losses, he can, in time, reorganize his life and move beyond the intensity of the initial pain. Some losses are, of course, so profound and so painful that a mourner is forever changed. But for Christians who place their faith completely in their Creator—and in His only begotten Son—the experience of grief is different in one very important respect: Christians face grief armed with God's promises.

Through the Holy Bible, God promises to comfort and heal those who call upon Him. And He promises that the grave is not a final resting place; it is, instead, merely a place of transition—a way station on the path to eternal life—for those who give their hearts to God's Son.

As you ponder the ideas contained in this book, think carefully about your own situation: your emotions, your thoughts, your experiences, and your pain. And as you do, think carefully about the ways that you're responding to your own particular losses. The more you understand about the grieving process—and the more you understand about your own grieving process—the better you can cope with its many twists and turns. But whatever the nature of your loss, always remember this overriding truth: God is with you, God is good, and you are protected.

FEELING NUMB?

If you've experienced a recent loss, especially a profound loss, you may be surprised not by the intensity of your emotions, but by the lack of them. If so, you should know that emotional numbness is a common response to any significant loss, especially in the early stages of the grieving process.

So, if you're feeling numb, don't think you're the only person who's ever felt that way. And if you're still in a state of disbelief, don't shut yourself off from your loved ones. Keep talking to your family, to your friends, and to God. When you do, you'll discover that talking about your grief, while painful at first, can be helpful in the long run.

SOMETHING TO REMEMBER

When you're hurting, it's up to you to find people who understand your pain and are willing to talk about it. Even if you're a person who usually keeps things bottled up inside, you'll be wise to talk about your feelings with trusted friends, with family members, and, most importantly, with God.

MORE FROM GOD'S WORD ABOUT GRIEF

God will wipe away every tear from their eyes.

Revelation 7:17 HCSB

When I sit in darkness, the Lord will be a light to me.

Micah 7:8 NKJV

Blessed are those who mourn, for they will be comforted.

Matthew 5:4 NIV

So you also have sorrow now. But I will see you again. Your hearts will rejoice, and no one will rob you of your joy.

John 16:22 HCSB

MORE POWERFUL IDEAS ABOUT GRIEF

God's Word never said we were not to grieve our losses. It says we are not to grieve as those who have no hope (1 Thessalonians 4:13). Big Difference.

Beth Moore

There is no pit so deep that God's love is not deeper still.

Corrie ten Boom

The kingdom of God is a kingdom of paradox, where through the ugly defeat of a cross, a holy God is utterly glorified. Victory comes through defeat; healing through brokenness; finding self through losing self.

Chuck Colson

Suffering is no argument of God's displeasure; it is simply a part of the fiber of our lives.

Fanny Crosby

When the full impact of our loss hit home, it seemed that everything moved in slow motion.

Zig Ziglar

Sorrow is a fruit; God does not make it grow on limbs too weak to bear it.

Victor Hugo

No one is immune from
the fact of grief.
Grief is woven throughout
the tapestry of life.

—

Zig Ziglar

In grief nothing "stays put." One keeps on emerging from a phase, but it always recurs. Round and round. Everything repeats. Am I going in circles, or dare I hope I am on a spiral?

C. S. Lewis

Grief is pervasive. You never get over it, but you learn to recognize and live with it.

Zig Ziglar

Grief. The pain now is part of the happiness then. That's the deal.

C. S. Lewis

While I do not believe that God causes the circumstances that result in our grief, I do believe that God uses grief as a process to show His compassion toward us, to teach us, and to bring us to greater wholeness.

Zig Ziglar

Pain is a fact of life in this fallen world, and so the goal in life is not to escape pain, but instead to triumph over it, while learning the lessons only pain can teach.

Charles Swindoll

QUESTIONS TO CONSIDER

Do I place my hopes in God?

_____

_____

Despite the pain that I am feeling today, do I sincerely believe that, with God's help, I can one day find relief from my suffering?

_____

_____

Do I place limitations on myself, and do I place limitations on God's power to heal me and to use me for His purposes?

_____

_____

A PRAYER FOR TODAY

*You have promised, Lord, that You will not give me
more than I can bear. You have promised to lift me out
of my grief and despair. You have promised to put
a new song on my lips. I thank You, Lord,
for sustaining me in my day of sorrow. Restore me,
and heal me, and use me as You will. Amen*

Day 4

HOW LONG?

I waited patiently for the LORD;
and He inclined to me, and heard my cry.

Psalm 40:1 NKJV

THE FOCUS FOR TODAY

There is no timetable on grief work.
Your grief time depends on the voltage of the relationship
you had with the person you lost, or the importance
of the dream that was not fulfilled.

Barbara Johnson

Once grieving begins, almost everyone wonders: "How long will it last?" There is no universal answer to this question. Different people grieve in different ways. You, therefore, will grieve at your own pace.

Mourning is a process that cannot be hurried; each significant loss is experienced and processed according to its own timetable. But in the darkness of your own particular sorrow, it is imperative to remember that God stands forever ready, offering His healing hand to you.

TRUST HIS TIMETABLE

The Bible teaches us to trust God's timing in all matters, but we are sorely tempted to do otherwise, especially when our hearts are breaking. We pray (and trust) that we will find peace some day, and we want it NOW. God, however, works on His own timetable, and His schedule does not always coincide with ours.

God's plans are perfect; ours most certainly are not. Thus we must learn to trust the Father in good times and hard times.

Elisabeth Elliot advised, "We must learn to move according to the timetable of the Timeless One, and to be at peace." So today, as you meet the challenges of everyday life, do your best to turn everything over to God. Whatever your problem, He can solve it. And you can be sure that He will solve it when the time is right.

SOMETHING TO REMEMBER

In time, God will dry your tears if you let Him: And if you haven't already allowed Him to begin His healing process, today is the perfect day to start. (Psalm 147:3)

MORE FROM GOD'S WORD ABOUT GOD'S TIMING

He [Jesus] said to them: "It is not for you to know the times or dates the Father has set by his own authority."

Acts 1:7 NIV

He has made everything beautiful in its time. He has also set eternity in the hearts of men; yet they cannot fathom what God has done from beginning to end.

Ecclesiastes 3:11 NIV

Yet the LORD longs to be gracious to you; he rises to show you compassion. For the LORD is a God of justice. Blessed are all who wait for him!

Isaiah 30:18 NIV

I wait for the LORD, my soul waits, and in his word I put my hope.

Psalm 130:5 NIV

Wait for the LORD; be strong and take heart and wait for the LORD.

Psalm 27:14 NIV

More Powerful Ideas About God's Timing

The best we can hope for in this life is a knothole peek at the shining realities ahead. Yet a glimpse is enough. It's enough to convince our hearts that whatever sufferings and sorrows currently assail us aren't worthy of comparison to that which waits over the horizon.

Joni Eareckson Tada

If you want to receive emotional healing from God and come into an area of wholeness, you must realize that healing is a process, and you must allow the Lord to deal with you and your problem in His own way and in His own time.

Joyce Meyer

As we wait on God, He helps us use the winds of adversity to soar above our problems. As the Bible says, "Those who wait on the LORD . . . shall mount up with wings like eagles."

Billy Graham

When God is silent, you have only one reasonable option—trust Him; hang in there; wait on Him. He may be quiet, but He has not quit on you.

Charles Stanley

By perseverance
the snail reached the ark.

—

C. H. Spurgeon

MORE POWERFUL IDEAS ABOUT PERSEVERANCE

Perseverance is more than endurance. It is endurance combined with absolute assurance and certainty that what we are looking for is going to happen.

Oswald Chambers

Press on. Obstacles are seldom the same size tomorrow as they are today.

Robert Schuller

In the Bible, patience is not a passive acceptance of circumstances. It is a courageous perseverance in the face of suffering and difficulty.

Warren Wiersbe

Battles are won in the trenches, in the grit and grime of courageous determination; they are won day by day in the arena of life.

Charles Swindoll

Only the man who follows the command of Jesus single-mindedly and unresistingly lets his yoke rest upon him, finds his burden easy, and under its gentle pressure receives the power to persevere in the right way.

Dietrich Bonhoeffer

QUESTIONS TO CONSIDER

Do I take seriously the Bible's instructions to be patient?

_____

_____

Do I believe that patience is not idle waiting but that it is an activity that means watching and waiting for God to lead me in the direction of His choosing?

_____

_____

Do I believe that in time God can—and will—heal my heart and lead me in a new direction?

_____

_____

A PRAYER FOR TODAY

Dear Lord, Your wisdom is infinite, and the timing of Your heavenly plan is perfect. You have a plan for my life that is grander than I can imagine.
When I am impatient, remind me that You are never early or late. You are always on time, Father, so let me trust in You. Amen

Day 5

ASK HIM

So I say to you, keep asking, and it will be given to you.
Keep searching, and you will find.
Keep knocking, and the door will be opened to you.
Luke 11:9 HCSB

THE FOCUS FOR TODAY

Don't be afraid to ask your Heavenly Father for anything
you need. Indeed, nothing is too small for God's
attention or too great for his power.

Dennis Swanberg

How often do you ask God for His help and His wisdom? Occasionally? Intermittently? Whenever you experience a crisis? Hopefully not. Hopefully, you've acquired the habit of asking for God's assistance early and often. And if you've acquired that habit, it will serve you well, especially when you experience the pangs of grief.

Jesus made it clear to His disciples: they should petition God to meet their needs. So should you. Genuine, heartfelt prayer has the potential to produce powerful changes in you and in your world.

God can help you begin the process of moving through and beyond your grief. He can dry your tears and calm your fears if you have the courage to ask Him (and the determination to keep asking Him). But when it comes to grief work (or any other kind of work, for that matter), please don't expect God to do it all; He intends for you to help. When you do your part, He will do His part—and when He does, you can expect miraculous results.

The Bible promises that God will guide you if you let Him. Your job is to let Him. God has promised that when you ask for His help, He will not withhold it. So ask. Ask Him to meet your needs moment by moment, day by day, week by week, and year by year. Ask Him to lead you, to protect you, to correct you, and to heal you.

God stands at the door and waits. When you knock, He opens. When you ask, He answers. Your task is to make God a full partner in every aspect of your life—in good times and hard times—and to seek His guidance prayerfully, confidently, and often.

ASK FOR HIS STRENGTH

Sometimes, when our hearts are breaking and the world seems to be crashing down around us, we forget to slow ourselves down long enough to talk with God. Instead of turning our thoughts and prayers to Him, we rely entirely upon our own resources, with decidedly mixed results. Or, instead of praying for strength, we seek to manufacture it within ourselves, only to find that lasting strength remains elusive.

Are you in need? Ask God to sustain you. And don't be afraid to ask for the loving support of your loved ones, too. When you ask for help, you'll receive it. So the next time you're in pain, remember that help is on the way . . . all you must do is ask.

SOMETHING TO REMEMBER

When you ask God for His assistance, He hears your request—and in His own time, He answers. If you need more, ask more.

MORE FROM GOD'S WORD ABOUT ASKING GOD

Do not worry about anything, but pray and ask God for everything you need, always giving thanks.

Philippians 4:6 NCV

Verily, verily, I say unto you, He that believeth on me, the works that I do shall he do also; and greater works than these shall he do; because I go unto my Father. And whatsoever ye shall ask in my name, that will I do, that the Father may be glorified in the Son. If ye shall ask any thing in my name, I will do it.

John 14:12-14 KJV

You did not choose me, but I chose you and appointed you to go and bear fruit—fruit that will last. Then the Father will give you whatever you ask in my name.

John 15:16 NIV

MORE POWERFUL IDEAS ABOUT ASKING GOD

The God of the galaxies is the God who knows when your heart is broken—and He can heal it!

Warren Wiersbe

You don't have to be alone in your hurt! Comfort is yours. Joy is an option. And it's all been made possible by your Savior. He went without comfort so you might have it. He postponed joy so you might share in it. He willingly chose isolation so you might never be alone in your hurt and sorrow.

Joni Eareckson Tada

When you ask God to do something, don't ask timidly; put your whole heart into it.

Marie T. Freeman

God will help us become the people we are meant to be, if only we will ask Him.

Hannah Whitall Smith

Some people think God does not like to be troubled with our constant asking. But, the way to trouble God is not to come at all.

D. L. Moody

QUESTIONS TO CONSIDER

When I am in pain, do I ask God for help?

_____

_____

When I am in need, do I ask for God's help—and keep asking—until He answers my prayers?

_____

_____

Have I acquired the habit of asking for God's help many times each day?

_____

_____

A PRAYER FOR TODAY

Dear Lord, when I grieve, I will turn to You.
When I am weak, I will seek Your strength.
When I am discouraged, Father, I will be mindful
of Your love and Your grace. I will ask You
for the things I need, Father, and I will trust
Your answers, today and forever. Amen

Day 6

THE POWER OF FAITH

Jesus answered them, "I assure you: If you have faith and do not doubt, you will not only do what was done to the fig tree, but even if you tell this mountain, 'Be lifted up and thrown into the sea,' it will be done."
Matthew 21:21 HCSB

THE FOCUS FOR TODAY

Despair is always the gateway of faith.
Oswald Chambers

Every significant loss carries with it significant pain, but grieving Christians find strength and comfort in their faith. Faith gives assurance in times of doubt; it provides courage during times of fear. During times of intense grief, wise Christians renew themselves through prayer, through worship, and through a careful study of God's Holy Word.

When a suffering woman sought healing by merely touching the hem of His cloak, Jesus replied, "Daughter, be of good comfort; thy faith hath made thee whole" (Matthew 9:22 KJV). Christ's message is clear: we should live by faith. But, when we face adversity, illness, or heartbreak, living by faith can be difficult indeed. Yet this much is certain: whatever our circumstances, we must continue to plant the seeds of faith in our hearts, trusting that, in time, God will bring forth a bountiful harvest.

Have you, on occasion, felt your faith in God slipping away? If so, consider yourself a member of a very large club. We human beings are subject to an assortment of negative emotions such as fear, worry, anxiety, and doubt. When we fall short of perfect faith, God understands us and forgives us. And God stands ready to strengthen us if we turn our doubts and fears over to Him.

As you enter into the next phase of your life—as you move through and beyond feelings of intense pain—you'll have good days and bad days. When the sun is shining and all is well, you'll find it easier to have faith. But, when the storm clouds form overhead and your emotions take an unexpected turn for the worse, your faith will be tested. In times of trouble and doubt, God remains faithful to you. Do the same for Him.

Are you tapped in to the power of faith? Hopefully so. The hours that you invest in Bible study, prayer, meditation, and worship can be times of comfort and restoration. And, if your faith is being tested to the point of breaking, know that your Savior is near. Reach out to Him, and let Him heal your broken spirit. Be content to touch even the smallest fragment of the Master's garment, and He will make you whole.

SOMETHING TO REMEMBER

Feelings come and feelings go, but God never changes. So when you have a choice between trusting your feelings or trusting God, trust God. And remember that if your faith is strong enough, you and God—working together—can heal your heart.

MORE FROM GOD'S WORD ABOUT GOD'S WORD

All Scripture is inspired by God and is profitable for teaching, for rebuking, for correcting, for training in righteousness, so that the man of God may be complete, equipped for every good work.

2 Timothy 3:16-17 HCSB

For the word of God is living and effective and sharper than any two-edged sword, penetrating as far as to divide soul, spirit, joints, and marrow; it is a judge of the ideas and thoughts of the heart.

Hebrews 4:12 HCSB

The one who is from God listens to God's words. This is why you don't listen, because you are not from God.

John 8:47 HCSB

For I am not ashamed of the gospel, because it is God's power for salvation to everyone who believes.

Romans 1:16 HCSB

Man shall not live by bread alone, but by every word that proceeds from the mouth of God.

Matthew 4:4 NKJV

MORE POWERFUL IDEAS ABOUT THE POWER OF FAITH

Trials and sufferings teach us to obey the Lord by faith, and we soon learn that obedience pays off in joyful ways.

Bill Bright

A faith that hasn't been tested can't be trusted.

Adrian Rogers

The closer we are to God, the more confidence we place in him when we are under fire.

C. H. Spurgeon

It has been the faith of the Son of God who loves me and gave Himself for me that has held me in the darkest valley and the hottest fires and the deepest waters.

Elisabeth Elliot

Throughout our months and years of grieving, faith has been the redeeming force that has enabled us to bear the pain.

Zig Ziglar

Faith does not concern itself with the entire journey. One step is enough.

Mrs. Charles E. Cowman

QUESTIONS TO CONSIDER

Despite my suffering, am I willing to ask God to become a full partner in my life?

_____

_____

Am I willing to pray as if everything depended upon God and work as if everything depended upon me?

_____

_____

Am I willing to trust God's sovereignty and His plan for my life, even when I am in pain?

_____

_____

A PRAYER FOR TODAY

Dear Lord, in the darkness of uncertainty, give me faith. In those moments when I am afraid, give me faith. When I grieve, strengthen my faith in You. You are the Good Shepherd, let me trust in the perfection of Your plan and in the salvation of Your Son, this day and every day of my life. Amen

Day 7

EXPERIENCING AND EXPRESSING YOUR EMOTIONS

Blessed are those who mourn, for they shall be comforted.
Matthew 5:4 NKJV

THE FOCUS FOR TODAY

Those who mourn are those who have allowed
themselves to feel real feelings because
they care about other people.
Barbara Johnson

In the Old Testament, Job's example teaches us that it's okay to express grief. Job cried bitter tears; he cursed the day he was born (Job 3:1-3); he expressed questions that he could not answer; and he gave voice to his suffering. But he never grieved alone. When everyone else failed him, including friends and family, Job knew that God still ruled over the entire world and over Job's own corner of the world. Job trusted that God was always present . . . and so should you.

God gave you emotions, and He intends for you to use them. When you express your emotions sincerely, you will begin the process of healing. But if you suppress your emotions or if you ignore your feelings altogether, you may needlessly prolong your pain.

So, if you have experienced a significant loss or a profound disappointment, don't bottle up everything inside. Express your feelings; talk openly to loved ones; allow tears to flow. Even if you'd rather ignore your pain, don't do it. Instead, reach out to the people you love and trust.

By honestly expressing your grief, you will take an active role in God's plan for your recovery. And in time, you'll experience the comfort and the joy that can—and should—be yours.

SOMETHING TO REMEMBER

Grief is not meant to be avoided or feared; it is meant to be worked through. Grief hurts, but denying your true feelings can hurt even more. With God's help, you can face your pain and move beyond it. (Psalm 118:5-6)

MORE FROM GOD'S WORD ABOUT EXPRESSING GRIEF

Peace I leave with you; My peace I give to you; not as the world gives do I give to you. Do not let your heart be troubled, nor let it be fearful.

John 14:27 NASB

But now you must also put away all the following: anger, wrath, malice, slander, and filthy language from your mouth.

Colossians 3:8 HCSB

All bitterness, anger and wrath, insult and slander must be removed from you, along with all wickedness. And be kind and compassionate to one another, forgiving one another, just as God also forgave you in Christ.

Ephesians 4:31-32 HCSB

My dear brothers and sisters, always be willing to listen and slow to speak. Do not become angry easily, because anger will not help you live the right kind of life God wants.

James 1:19-20 NCV

And the peace of God, which surpasses all comprehension, will guard your hearts and your minds in Christ Jesus.

Philippians 4:7 NASB

MORE POWERFUL IDEAS ABOUT EXPRESSING GRIEF

There is no way around suffering. We have to go through it to get to the other side.

Barbara Johnson

Mercy is not the ability to no longer feel the pain and heartache of living in this world. Mercy is knowing that I am being held through the pain by my Father.

Angela Thomas

Researchers have been learning that people who cry frequently enjoy better health overall.

Barbara Johnson

If we are not willing to feel negative emotions, then we shall not experience the richness of our positive emotions.

C. S. Lewis

Christians are told not to stifle their grief or to behave unscripturally stoic.

Charles Stanley

When we cry, we allow our bodies to function according to God's design—and we embrace one of the "perks" he offers to relieve our stress.

Barbara Johnson

QUESTIONS TO CONSIDER

Am I willing to express my emotions, or do I keep my feelings bottled up inside?

_____

_____

Do I have trusted friends and family members with whom I can share my feelings?

_____

_____

Am I willing to express my feelings to God, and when I am in pain, do I ask Him to heal my heart?

_____

_____

A PRAYER FOR TODAY

Dear Lord, when I am heartbroken, I will share my grief with You. And I will share my feelings with trusted friends and family members. I will open my heart to You, Father, and to trusted friends who can give me comfort and hope. Amen

UNDERSTANDING DEPRESSION

My soul is weary of my life.
Job 10:1 KJV

THE FOCUS FOR TODAY

Feelings of uselessness and hopelessness
are not from God, but from the evil one, the devil,
who wants to discourage you
and thwart your effectiveness for the Lord.

Bill Bright

It has been said, and with good reason, that depression is the common cold of mental illness. Why? Because depression is such a common malady. But make no mistake: depression is a serious condition that, if untreated, can take a terrible toll on individuals and families alike.

The sadness that accompanies any significant loss is an inescapable fact of life. Throughout our lives, all of us must endure the kinds of deep personal losses that leave us struggling to find hope. But in time, we move beyond our grief as the sadness runs its course and gradually abates.

Depression, on the other hand, is a physical and emotional condition that is, in almost all cases, treatable with medication and counseling. Depression is not a disease to be taken lightly. Left untreated, it presents real dangers to patients' physical health and to their emotional well-being.

If you find yourself feeling "blue," perhaps it's a logical reaction to the ups and downs of daily life. But if your feelings of sadness have lasted longer than you think they should—or if someone close to you fears that your sadness may have evolved into clinical depression—it's time to seek professional help.

Here are a few simple guidelines to consider as you make decisions about possible medical treatment: 1. If you have persistent urges toward self-destructive behavior, or if you feel as though you have lost the will to live, consult a professional counselor or physician immediately. 2. If someone you trust urges you to seek counseling, schedule a session with a professionally trained counselor to evaluate your condition. 3. If you experience persistent and prolonged changes in sleep patterns, or if you experience a significant change in weight (either gain or loss), consult your physician. 4. If you are plagued by consistent, prolonged, severe feelings of hopelessness, consult a physician, a professional counselor, or your pastor.

In the familiar words of John 10:10, Jesus promises, "I have come that they may have life, and that they may have it more abundantly" (NKJV). And in John 15:11, He states, "These things I have spoken to you, that My joy may remain in you, and that your joy may be full." These two passages make it clear: our Savior intends that we experience lives of joyful abundance through Him. Our duty, as grateful believers, is to do everything we can to receive the joy and abundance that can be ours in Christ—and the term "everything" includes appropriate medical treatment when necessary.

Some days are light and happy, and some days are not. When we face the inevitable dark days of life, we must choose how we will respond. Will we allow ourselves to sink even more deeply into our own sadness, or will we do the difficult work of pulling ourselves out? We bring light to the dark days of life by turning first to God, and then to trusted family members, to friends, and, in some cases, to medical professionals. When we do, the clouds will eventually part, and the sun will shine once more upon our souls.

SOMETHING TO REMEMBER

Depression is serious business, and it's a highly treatable disease . . . treat it that way.

MORE POWERFUL IDEAS ABOUT DEPRESSION

What the devil loves is that vague cloud of unspecified guilt feeling or unspecified virtue by which he lures us into despair or presumption.

C. S. Lewis

Emotions we have not poured out in the safe hands of God can turn into feelings of hopelessness and depression. God is safe.

Beth Moore

Self blame over the past leads to depression in the present and poor decisions for the future.

Barbara Johnson

I was learning something important: we are most vulnerable to the piercing winds of doubt when we distance ourselves from the mission and fellowship to which Christ has called us. Our night of discouragement will seem endless and our task impossible, unless we recognize that He stands in our midst.

Joni Eareckson Tada

To lose heart is to lose everything.

John Eldredge

QUESTIONS TO CONSIDER

When I feel emotional pain, do I ignore it or address it?

_____

_____

If I have persistent feelings of sadness or despair—or if I know somebody who does—am I willing to seek help immediately?

_____

_____

Do I have friends and family members whom I can trust to tell me when I might need to see a trained counselor or physician? And will I listen to the advice?

_____

_____

A PRAYER FOR TODAY

Lord, You have promised to lift me up from the pit of my despair, and You have promised to place a new song on my lips. If the darkness envelops me, remind me of those promises. And, give me the wisdom to accept help from the people You have placed along my path. Amen

Day 9

GUARDING YOUR THOUGHTS

Finally brothers, whatever is true, whatever is honorable,
whatever is just, whatever is pure, whatever is lovely,
whatever is commendable—if there is any moral excellence
and if there is any praise—dwell on these things.
Philippians 4:8 HCSB

THE FOCUS FOR TODAY

Part of every misery is, so to speak, the misery's shadow
or reflection: the fact that you don't merely suffer but
that you have to keep on thinking about the fact that you
suffer. I not only live each endless day in grief, but I live
each day thinking about living each day in grief.

C. S. Lewis

I f you've been plagued by intense feelings of grief, nobody needs to tell you that thoughts are intensely powerful things—you know from personal experience.

Our thoughts have the power to lift us up or drag us down; they have the power to energize us or deplete us, to inspire us to greater accomplishments, or to make those accomplishments impossible.

Bishop Fulton Sheen correctly observed, "The mind is like a clock that is constantly running down. It needs to be wound up daily with good thoughts." But sometimes, even for the most faithful believers, winding up our intellectual clocks is difficult indeed. Difficult, but necessary.

So if negative feelings have left you worried, exhausted, or both, it's time to readjust your thought patterns by training yourself to focus more on God's power and on your own possibilities. Both are far greater than you can imagine.

BEYOND SELF-PITY

If you're enduring the pangs of grief, you may be plagued by feelings of self-pity. But here's a word of warning: Self-pity is not only an unproductive way to think; it is also an affront to your Father in heaven.

Self-pity and thanksgiving cannot coexist in the same mind. Bitterness and joy cannot coexist in the same heart. Gratitude and despair are mutually exclusive.

So even if you've experienced a heartbreaking loss, don't allow pain and regret to dominate your life. As you move through and beyond your grief, you can—and should—train yourself to think less about your pain and more about God's love. Focus your mind on Him, and let your sorrows fend for themselves.

SOMETHING TO REMEMBER

Watch what you think. If your inner voice is like a broken record that keeps repeating negative thoughts, you must guard your heart more carefully. And while you're at it, you should train yourself to begin thinking thoughts that are more rational, more positive, more forgiving, and less destructive.

MORE FROM GOD'S WORD ABOUT YOUR THOUGHTS

So prepare your minds for service and have self-control.

1 Peter 1:13 NCV

Come near to God, and God will come near to you. You sinners, clean sin out of your lives. You who are trying to follow God and the world at the same time, make your thinking pure.

James 4:8 NCV

Those who are pure in their thinking are happy, because they will be with God.

Matthew 5:8 NCV

Dear friend, guard Clear Thinking and Common Sense with your life; don't for a minute lose sight of them. They'll keep your soul alive and well, they'll keep you fit and attractive.

Proverbs 3:21-22 MSG

May the words of my mouth and the thoughts of my heart be pleasing to you, O LORD, my rock and my redeemer.

Psalm 19:14 NLT

MORE POWERFUL IDEAS ABOUT YOUR THOUGHTS

The mind is like a clock that is constantly running down.
It has to be wound up daily with good thoughts.

Fulton J. Sheen

As we have by faith said no to sin, so we should by faith
say yes to God and set our minds on things above, where
Christ is seated in the heavenlies.

Vonette Bright

No more imperfect thoughts. No more sad memories. No
more ignorance. My redeemed body will have a redeemed
mind. Grant me a foretaste of that perfect mind as you
mirror your thoughts in me today.

Joni Eareckson Tada

It is the thoughts and intents of the heart that shape a
person's life.

John Eldredge

Attitude is the mind's paintbrush; it can color any
situation.

Barbara Johnson

QUESTIONS TO CONSIDER

Do I understand the importance of directing my thoughts in a proper direction?

_____

_____

Do I believe that emotions are contagious, and do I try to associate with people who are optimistic, hopeful, and encouraging?

_____

_____

Do I understand that when I dwell on negative aspects of my past, I feel worse, and that when I focus on my blessings, I feel better?

_____

_____

A PRAYER FOR TODAY
*Dear Lord, I will focus on Your love, Your promises,
and Your Son. When I am weak, I will turn to You
for strength; when I am worried, I will turn to You for
comfort and perspective. Help me guard my thoughts,
Lord, so that I may honor You always. Amen*

Day 10

ACCEPTING ENCOURAGEMENT AND ADVICE

Listen to advice and accept correction,
and in the end you will be wise.
Proverbs 19:20 NCV

THE FOCUS FOR TODAY

God often keeps us on the path by guiding us through
the counsel of friends and trusted spiritual advisors.
Bill Hybels

If your world has been turned upside down—or shattered—you should reach out to trusted friends and family members who have truly walked in your shoes—men and women who have experienced your particular pain and lived to tell about it. And then, when you've recruited a small team of friends and counselors, it's time for you to talk (about your feelings) and listen (to their advice).

God doesn't intend for you to suffer in solitude, so He inevitably places counselors and comforters along your path. But when you're hurting, it's tempting to pull the drapes, to lock the door, to take the phone off the hook, and to sit, alone, in your self-pity. Tempting, but unwise. A far better way to deal with your feelings is to share them with the folks whom God sends your way.

So, the next time you're tempted to wall yourself off inside an emotional prison of your own making, resist that temptation. Instead, find a compassionate friend you can talk to or pray with, or even cry with. Consider that friend to be God's gift to you—a precious gift you can use to guide your path and hasten your healing.

DEPEND ON LOYAL CHRISTIAN FRIENDS

Loyal Christian friends have much to offer us: encouragement, faith, and fellowship, for starters. And, if our hearts are heavy, our friends offer us comfort, perspective, and hope. When we align ourselves with godly believers, we are blessed by them and by our Creator.

As you seek to move beyond the heartbreaks of the past, remember the important role that Christian friendship plays in God's plans for His kingdom and for your recovery. God wants to help you empty your heart of sadness so that He can fill it with joy. And talking things over with fellow believers can help.

SOMETHING TO REMEMBER

Whether you realize it or not, there are plenty of people who want to offer you encouragement, comfort, and support. Your job is to find them . . . and to let them help.

MORE FROM GOD'S WORD ABOUT
ACCEPTING WISE COUNSEL

Arrogance leads to nothing but strife, but wisdom is gained by those who take advice.

Proverbs 13:10 HCSB

The way of a fool is right in his own eyes, but he who heeds counsel is wise.

Proverbs 12:15 NKJV

Listen to good advice if you want to live well, an honored guest among wise men and women.

Proverbs 15:31 MSG

Mockers don't love those who rebuke them, so they stay away from the wise.

Proverbs 15:12 NLT

The wise are glad to be instructed.

Proverbs 10:8 NLT

MORE POWERFUL IDEAS ABOUT ENCOURAGING FRIENDS AND MENTORS

The man who never reads will never be read; he who never quotes will never be quoted. He who will not use the thoughts of other men's brains proves that he has no brains of his own.

C. H. Spurgeon

The next best thing to being wise oneself is to live in a circle of those who are.

C. S. Lewis

The effective mentor strives to help a man or woman discover what they can be in Christ and then holds them accountable to become that person.

Howard Hendricks

Yes, the Spirit was sent to be our Counselor. Yes, Jesus speaks to us personally. But often he works through another human being.

John Eldredge

You can't light another's path without casting light on your own.

John Maxwell

QUESTIONS TO CONSIDER

When friends and family members offer me comfort and encouragement, do I listen carefully, or do I brush them off?

_____

_____

Do I seek out people who are uplifting and upbeat, or do I usually associate with folks who tend to be less positive and more cynical?

_____

_____

Am I a source of encouragement to others, and do I allow others to be a source of encouragement to me?

_____

_____

A PRAYER FOR TODAY

Dear Lord, thank You for the comforting friends You have placed along my path. When I am troubled, let me turn to them for help, for guidance, for hope, and for perspective. And Father, let me be a friend to others, so that my love for You may be demonstrated by my genuine concern for them. Amen

Day 11

NEVER ALONE

Do not be afraid or discouraged.
For the LORD your God is with you wherever you go.

Joshua 1:9 NLT

THE FOCUS FOR TODAY

Are you feeling lonely today because of suffering?
My word to you is simply this:
Jesus Christ is there with you.

Warren Wiersbe

Perhaps you feel alone in your grief. Perhaps you feel like you've been isolated by events and circumstances from which you can never recover. If you have these feelings—and even if these feelings seem very real indeed—you're mistaken. You're never really alone because God is always with you. God is everywhere we have ever been and everywhere we will ever be.

When we turn to God often, we are blessed by His presence. But, if we ignore the Lord's presence or rebel against it altogether, the world in which we live soon becomes a spiritual wasteland.

Since God is everywhere, we are free to sense His presence whenever we take the time to quiet our souls and turn our prayers to Him. But sometimes, amid the incessant demands of everyday life, we turn our thoughts far from God; when we do, we suffer.

Are you exhausted, discouraged, or fearful? Be comforted because God is with you. Are you confused? Listen to the quiet voice of your Heavenly Father. Are you bitter? Talk with God and seek His guidance. Are you still grieving a loss from long ago? Ask God to heal your heart. He is the Giver of all things good. So in whatever condition you find yourself—whether you are happy or sad, victorious or vanquished, troubled or triumphant—acknowledge His presence.

SILENCE IS INDEED GOLDEN

As you struggle to regain your footing after any significant loss, you may become so wrapped up in your daily obligations that you fail to spend quiet time with God. And that's a big mistake.

When you are suffering, you desperately need God. So you should carve out a quiet time each day to experience the Father's peace and His love. When you do, God will touch your heart, He will restore your spirits, and He will give you perspective. If you really want to know your Heavenly Father—and if you want to partake in His peace—silence is a wonderful place to start.

SOMETHING TO REMEMBER

When you grieve, God remains steadfast . . . and He can comfort you if you let Him. Let Him.

MORE FROM GOD'S WORD ABOUT GOD'S PRESENCE

Come near to God, and God will come near to you. You sinners, clean sin out of your lives. You who are trying to follow God and the world at the same time, make your thinking pure.

James 4:8 NCV

For the eyes of the Lord range throughout the earth to strengthen those whose hearts are fully committed to him.

2 Chronicles 16:9 NIV

Fear not, for I am with you; Be not dismayed, for I am your God. I will strengthen you.

Isaiah 41:10 NKJV

Surely goodness and mercy shall follow me all the days of my life: and I will dwell in the house of the Lord for ever.

Psalm 23:6 KJV

I am not alone, because the Father is with Me.

John 16:32 HCSB

More from God's Word About God's Peace

I leave you peace; my peace I give you. I do not give it to you as the world does. So don't let your hearts be troubled or afraid.

John 14:27 NCV

And the peace of God, which surpasses all understanding, will guard your hearts and minds through Christ Jesus. Finally, brethren, whatever things are true, whatever things are noble, whatever things are just, whatever things are pure, whatever things are lovely, whatever things are of good report, if there is any virtue and if there is anything praiseworthy—meditate on these things.

Philippians 4:7-8 NKJV

Blessed are the peacemakers, for they will be called sons of God.

Matthew 5:9 NIV

I have told you these things so that in Me you may have peace. In the world you have suffering. But take courage! I have conquered the world.

John 16:33 HCSB

Be of good comfort, be of one mind, live in peace; and the God of love and peace will be with you.

2 Corinthians 13:11 NKJV

MORE POWERFUL IDEAS ABOUT GOD'S PRESENCE

Though our pain and our disappointment and the details of our suffering may differ, there is an abundance of God's grace and peace available to each of us.

Charles Swindoll

We all go through pain and sorrow, but the presence of God, like a warm, comforting blanket, can shield us and protect us, and allow the deep inner joy to surface, even in the most devastating circumstances.

Barbara Johnson

God whispers to us in our pleasures, speaks in our conscience, but shouts in our pain.

C. S. Lewis

Often, in the midst of great problems, we stop short of the real blessing God has for us, which is a fresh vision of who He is.

Anne Graham Lotz

God walks with us. He scoops us up in His arms or simply sits with us in silent strength until we cannot avoid the awesome recognition that yes, even now, He is here.

Gloria Gaither

MORE POWERFUL IDEAS ABOUT GOD'S PEACE

Thou hast formed us for Thyself, and our hearts are restless till they find rest in Thee.

St. Augustine

Peace is the deepest thing a human personality can know; it is almighty.

Oswald Chambers

What peace can they have who are not at peace with God?

Matthew Henry

God has promised us abundance, peace, and eternal life. These treasures are ours for the asking; all we must do is claim them. One of the great mysteries of life is why on earth do so many of us wait so very long to claim them?

Marie T. Freeman

God is in control of history; it's His story. Doesn't that give you a great peace—especially when world events seem so tumultuous and insane?

Kay Arthur

QUESTIONS TO CONSIDER

Do I believe that God seeks a close and intimate relationship with me?

_____

_____

Do I understand that whenever I feel distance from God, that distance is my own doing, not His?

_____

_____

Am I willing to quiet myself long enough to sense God's presence and His love?

_____

_____

A PRAYER FOR TODAY

Heavenly Father, even when it seems to me that You are far away, You never leave my side. Today and every day, I will strive to feel Your presence, and I will strive to sense Your love for me. Amen

Day 12

FEELING ANGRY?

Those who control their anger have great understanding;
those with a hasty temper will make mistakes.
Proverbs 14:29 NLT

THE FOCUS FOR TODAY

I am sure it is never sadness—a proper, straight, natural
response to loss—that does people harm, but all the other
things, all the resentment, dismay, doubt, and self-pity
with which it is usually complicated.

C. S. Lewis

The experience of grief is often accompanied by the emotions of anger and guilt. We are understandably angry about our losses, and we may feel guilty about the things that we might have done to prevent them. But please beware: prolonged feelings of anger or guilt have the potential to do you great harm.

Anger, left unchecked, tends to invade every aspect of life, eventually transforming itself into bitterness. Irrational guilt, especially over past events that cannot be changed, creates an environment of self-doubt and self-recrimination.

If you are ruled by feelings of anger, guilt, jealousy, fear, or any other negative emotion, understand that these emotions are part of the grieving process. But understand too that hurtful feelings should never become a permanent part of your emotional makeup. God has better things in store for you!

BITTERNESS IS POISON

Bitterness is a spiritual sickness. It will consume your soul; it is dangerous to your emotional health. It can destroy you if you let it . . . so don't let it!

If you are caught up in intense feelings of anger or resentment, you know all too well the destructive power of these emotions. How can you rid yourself of these feelings? First, you must prayerfully ask God to cleanse your heart. Then, you must learn to catch yourself whenever thoughts of bitterness or hatred begin to attack you. Your challenge is this: You must learn to resist negative thoughts before they hijack your emotions.

When you learn to direct your thoughts toward more positive (and rational) topics, you'll be protected from the spiritual and emotional consequences of bitterness . . . and you'll be wiser, healthier, and happier, too. So why wait? Defeat destructive bitterness today.

SOMETHING TO REMEMBER

Anger, if allowed to fester, can rob you of contentment and peace. So if you find yourself becoming a prisoner of chronic anger, it's time to ask God (sincerely and often) to heal your heart.

MORE FROM GOD'S WORD ABOUT ANGER

When you are angry, do not sin, and be sure to stop being angry before the end of the day. Do not give the devil a way to defeat you.

Ephesians 4:26–27 NCV

Everyone should be quick to listen, slow to speak and slow to become angry, for man's anger does not bring about the righteous life that God desires.

James 1:19-20 NIV

But I tell you that men will have to give account on the day of judgment for every careless word they have spoken. For by your words you will be acquitted, and by your words you will be condemned.

Matthew 12:36-37 NIV

I want men everywhere to lift up holy hands in prayer, without anger or disputing.

1 Timothy 2:8 NIV

Don't become angry quickly, because getting angry is foolish.

Ecclesiastes 7:9 NCV

MORE POWERFUL IDEAS ABOUT ANGER

Life is too short to spend it being angry, bored, or dull.

Barbara Johnson

When you strike out in anger, you may miss the other person, but you will always hit yourself.

Jim Gallery

Why lose your temper if, by doing so, you offend God, annoy other people, give yourself a bad time . . . and, in the end, have to find it again?

Josemaria Escriva

Is there somebody who's always getting your goat? Talk to the Shepherd.

Anonymous

Get rid of the poison of built-up anger and the acid of long-term resentment.

Charles Swindoll

QUESTIONS TO CONSIDER

When I am beset by feelings of anger, do I take those feelings to God and try my best to leave them there?

_____

_____

Do I understand the need to accept my past and forgive those who have hurt me?

_____

_____

Do I understand that peace and bitterness cannot coexist in my heart?

_____

_____

A PRAYER FOR TODAY
Dear Lord, help me to turn away from angry thoughts.
Today and every day, help me to use Jesus as my guide
for life, and let me trust His promises
today and forever. Amen

Day 13

ARE YOU FOCUSED ON WHAT WOULD, COULD, OR SHOULD HAVE BEEN?

And don't be wishing you were someplace else or with someone else. Where you are right now is God's place for you. Live and obey and love and believe right there.

1 Corinthians 7:17 MSG

THE FOCUS FOR TODAY

Even in long-term grief there is a way to bring closure and to rise above the rage, the guilt, the pain.
In Christ this is possible.

Barbara Johnson

Sometimes, we focus so intently on the things we could have done or should have done that we fail to focus on the present—and we fail to plan for the future. Instead of accepting God's sovereignty and making peace with the past, we think long and hard—far too long and hard—about the things that "might have been," the things that "could have been," or the things that "should have been."

Are you troubled by feelings of guilt, even after you've received God's forgiveness? Are you still struggling with painful memories of mistakes you made long ago? Are you focused so intently on yesterday that your vision of today is clouded? If so you still have work to do—spiritual work. You should ask your Heavenly Father not for forgiveness (He granted that gift the very first time you asked Him!) but instead for acceptance and trust: acceptance of the past and trust in God's plan for your life.

If you find yourself constantly plagued by feelings of guilt or regret, consult God's survival guide: His Holy Word. Become more diligent in your daily time of prayer and Bible study. When you do, you'll discover that a regular time of quiet reflection and prayer will allow you to praise your Creator, to focus your thoughts, to remind yourself of His love, and to seek His guidance in matters great and small.

BEYOND REGRET

Are you caught in the quicksand of regret? Are you bound up by the bonds of bitterness? Do you find it impossible to forgive others for the wrongs they may have done to you? If so, be forewarned: you are not only disobeying your Heavenly Father, but you are also harming your loved ones and yourself.

If you are caught up in intense feelings of anger or resentment, you know all too well the destructive power of these emotions. How can you rid yourself of these feelings? First, you must prayerfully ask God to cleanse your heart. Then, you must learn to catch yourself whenever feelings of anger or bitterness invade your thoughts. In short, you must learn to recognize and to resist negative thoughts before they hijack your emotions.

If there exists even one person—alive or dead—against whom you hold bitter feelings, it's time to forgive. Or, if you are embittered against yourself for some past mistake or shortcoming, it's finally time to forgive yourself and move on. Remember that bitterness is not part of God's plan for your life, so pray, think, and forgive accordingly.

SOMETHING TO REMEMBER

Avoid self-pity and renounce regret. Feeling sorry for yourself is a waste of precious time and energy; regretting the mistakes of yesterday won't help you build a better tomorrow.

MORE FROM GOD'S WORD ABOUT
GOD'S FORGIVENESS

It will be hard when all these things happen to you. But after that you will come back to the Lord your God and obey him, because the Lord your God is a merciful God. He will not leave you or destroy you. He will not forget the Agreement with your ancestors, which he swore to them.

Deuteronomy 4:30-31 NCV

But God's mercy is great, and he loved us very much. Though we were spiritually dead because of the things we did against God, he gave us new life with Christ. You have been saved by God's grace.

Ephesians 2:4-5 NCV

MORE POWERFUL IDEAS ABOUT GOD'S FORGIVENESS

The pardon of God deletes past, present, and future sins—completely!

Franklin Graham

Because his mercies are new every morning, you can find the courage to bring all of who you are to all of who he is.

Sheila Walsh

There is only One who can cleanse us from our sins—He who made us.

Corrie ten Boom

Mistakes offer the possibility for redemption and a new start in God's kingdom. No matter what you're guilty of, God can restore your innocence.

Barbara Johnson

To be righteous means to be in right standing with God because your sins have been taken care of!

Kay Arthur

Mercy is an attribute of God, an infinite and inexhaustible energy within the divine nature which disposes God to be actively compassionate.

A. W. Tozer

QUESTIONS TO CONSIDER

When I am overcome by feelings of regret, do I take those feelings to God and try my best to leave them there?

_____

_____

Do I understand the need to accept my past, even if the past is hurtful?

_____

_____

Do I understand that in order to achieve peace, I must make peace with the past?

_____

_____

A PRAYER FOR TODAY
Heavenly Father, free me from regret, resentment, and anger. When I am bitter, I cannot feel the peace that You intend for my life. Keep me mindful that forgiveness is Your commandment, and help me accept the past, treasure the present, and trust the future to You. Amen

Day 14

MARSHALING
YOUR RESOURCES

A wise man will hear and increase learning,
and a man of understanding will attain wise counsel.
Proverbs 1:5 NKJV

THE FOCUS FOR TODAY

Friendships are living organisms at work.
They continue to unfold, change, and emerge.
Barbara Johnson

As you work through your grief, you will find it helpful to utilize all the resources that are available to you. God intends that you have a meaningful, abundant life, but He expects you to do your part in claiming His blessings. Thus, it is your responsibility to seek out help when you need it. First and foremost, lean upon the love, help, and support of family, friends, fellow church members, and your pastor. Other resources include:

1. Various local counseling services including, but not limited to, pastoral counselors, psychologists, and community mental health facilities.

2. Group counseling programs which may deal with your specific loss. Talking with others who have experienced a loss similar to yours will be extremely helpful.

3. Your personal physician. The local bookstore or library (which will contain specific reading material about your grief and about your particular loss).

So if you're grieving, don't grieve alone. And whatever you do, don't convince yourself that your situation is helpless. In truth, help is as near as your telephone. Use it.

SOMETHING TO REMEMBER

Other people have experienced grief that is similar to yours, and they are willing to help: let them. (Matthew 5:4)

Trust is the soil in which the flower of friendship grows.

—

Marie T. Freeman

MORE FROM GOD'S WORD ABOUT FRIENDS

Beloved, if God so loved us, we also ought to love one another.

1 John 4:11 NKJV

Greater love has no one than this, that he lay down his life for his friends.

John 15:13 NIV

I thank my God upon every remembrance of you.

Philippians 1:3 NKJV

A friend loves at all times, and a brother is born for adversity.

Proverbs 17:17 NIV

Iron sharpeneth iron; so a man sharpeneth the countenance of his friend.

Proverbs 27:17 KJV

MORE POWERFUL IDEAS ABOUT FRIENDS

The glory of friendship is not the outstretched hand, or the kindly smile, or the joy of companionship. It is the spiritual inspiration that comes to one when he discovers that someone else believes in him and is willing to trust him with his friendship.

Corrie ten Boom

True friendship can harbor no suspicion; a friend must speak to a friend as freely as to his second self.

St. Jerome

Becoming a good friend is aerobic in that it takes time and effort. We don't just wake up one day, and voila: we are Wonder Friend!

Patsy Clairmont

Friendship fills a deep well within me with fresh water. When I celebrate my friendships, it's like dropping a huge rock into the well. It splashes that water everywhere, on everyone else in my life.

Nicole Johnson

QUESTIONS TO CONSIDER

Do I understand the importance of finding—and listening to—people who can comfort me?

_____

_____

As I work through the process of grieving, do I talk to friends, to family members, to mentors, and, most importantly, to God?

_____

_____

Am I willing to listen carefully to advice and, when appropriate, do I take it?

_____

_____

A PRAYER FOR TODAY

Lord, thank You for the friends, mentors, and counselors You have placed along my path. When I am troubled, let me turn to them for help, for guidance, for comfort, and for perspective. And let me be a friend and mentor to others, so that my love for You may be demonstrated by my genuine concern for them. Amen

Day 15

STUDYING HIS WORD, TRUSTING HIS PROMISES

All Scripture is inspired by God and is profitable for teaching,
for rebuking, for correcting, for training in righteousness,
so that the man of God may be complete,
equipped for every good work.
2 Timothy 3:16-17 HCSB

THE FOCUS FOR TODAY

The Bible is a Christian's guidebook, and I believe the
knowledge it sheds on pain and suffering is the great
antidote to fear for suffering people. Knowledge can
dissolve fear as light destroys darkness.

Philip Yancey

The words of Matthew 4:4 remind us that, "Man shall not live by bread alone but by every word that proceedeth out of the mouth of God" (KJV). As believers, we must study the Bible and meditate upon its meaning for our lives. Otherwise, we deprive ourselves of a priceless gift from our Creator.

God's Word is unlike any other book. The Bible is a roadmap for life here on earth and for life eternal. As Christians, we are called upon to study God's Holy Word, to follow its commandments, and to share its Good News with the world.

Jonathan Edwards advised, "Be assiduous in reading the Holy Scriptures. This is the fountain whence all knowledge in divinity must be derived. Therefore let not this treasure lie by you neglected." God's Holy Word is, indeed, a priceless, one-of-a-kind treasure, and a passing acquaintance with the Good Book is insufficient for Christians who seek to obey God's Word and to understand His will. After all, man does not live by bread alone . . .

GOD'S WORD OFFERS COMFORT

If you're experiencing the pains of a significant loss, God's promises offer comfort. And if you'd like to experience God's peace, Bible study can help provide it.

Warren Wiersbe observed, "When the child of God looks into the Word of God, he sees the Son of God. And, he is transformed by the Spirit of God to share in the glory of God." God's Holy Word is, indeed, a life-changing, spirit-lifting, one-of-a-kind treasure. And it's up to you—and only you—to use it that way.

SOMETHING TO REMEMBER

Never stop studying God's Word. Even if you've been studying the Bible for many years, you've still got lots to learn. Bible study should be a lifelong endeavor; make it your lifelong endeavor.

MORE FROM GOD'S WORD ABOUT GOD'S WORD

For the word of God is living and effective and sharper than any two-edged sword, penetrating as far as to divide soul, spirit, joints, and marrow; it is a judge of the ideas and thoughts of the heart.

Hebrews 4:12 HCSB

The one who is from God listens to God's words. This is why you don't listen, because you are not from God.

John 8:47 HCSB

For I am not ashamed of the gospel, because it is God's power for salvation to everyone who believes.

Romans 1:16 HCSB

Man shall not live by bread alone, but by every word that proceeds from the mouth of God.

Matthew 4:4 NKJV

But the word of the Lord endures forever. And this is the word that was preached as the gospel to you.

1 Peter 1:25 HCSB

MORE POWERFUL IDEAS ABOUT
THE POWER OF GOD'S WORD

The promises of God's Word sustain us in our suffering, and we know Jesus sympathizes and empathizes with us in our darkest hour.

Bill Bright

If you learn to trust God with a child-like dependence on Him as your loving Heavenly Father, no trouble can destroy you.

Billy Graham

Weave the fabric of God's Word through your heart and mind. It will hold strong, even if the rest of life unravels.

Gigi Graham Tchividjian

The Bible became a living book and a guide for my life.

Vonette Bright

Prayer and the Word are inseparably linked together. Power in the use of either depends on the presence of the other.

Andrew Murray

QUESTIONS TO CONSIDER

Do I make it a priority to read the Bible every day?

_____

_____

Do I consider regular Bible study to be an important source of wisdom?

_____

_____

Do I have a systematic plan for studying God's Word?

_____

_____

A PRAYER FOR TODAY

As I journey through this life, Lord, help me always to consult the true road map: Your Holy Word. I know that when I turn my heart and my thoughts to You, Father, You will lead me along the path that is right for me. Today, Dear Lord, let me know Your will and study Your Word so that I might know Your plan for my life. Amen

Day 16

WHEN FORGIVENESS IS HARD

For if you forgive people their wrongdoing, your heavenly Father will forgive you as well. But if you don't forgive people, your Father will not forgive your wrongdoing.
Matthew 6:14-15 HCSB

THE FOCUS FOR TODAY

As you have received the mercy of God by the forgiveness of sin and the promise of eternal life, thus you must show mercy.
Billy Graham

Do you invest more time than you should reliving the past? Is your grief complicated by feelings of anger, bitterness, or regret? Do you harbor ill will against someone whom you simply can't seem to forgive? If so, it's time to finally get serious about putting the past in its proper place: behind you.

When someone hurts you, the act of forgiveness is difficult, but necessary. Until you forgive, you are trapped in a prison of your own creation. But what if you have tried to forgive and simply can't seem to do so? The solution to your dilemma is this: you simply must make forgiveness a higher priority in your life.

Forgiveness is an exercise in spiritual growth: the more we forgive, the more we grow. Conversely, bitterness makes spiritual growth impossible: when our hearts are filled with resentment and anger, there is no room left for love.

In those quiet moments when we open our hearts to God, the Creator who made us keeps remaking us. He gives us direction, perspective, and wisdom—and He gives us the courage to forgive other folks sooner rather than later, which, by the way, is exactly what we should do. Most of us don't spend too much time thinking about forgiveness; we worry, instead, about the injustices we have suffered and the people who inflicted them. God has a better plan: He wants us to live in the present, not the past, and He knows that in order to do so, we must forgive those who have harmed us. Now.

MAKE FORGIVENESS A HIGH PRIORITY

If you're unwilling to forgive other people, you're building a roadblock between yourself and God. That's why you must make the task of forgiving everybody (including yourself) a high priority.

Forgiveness is a choice. We can either choose to forgive those who have injured us, or not. When we follow God's teachings by offering forgiveness to other people, we are blessed. But when we allow bitterness and resentment to poison our hearts, we are tortured by our own shortsightedness.

Do you harbor resentment against anyone? If so, you are faced with an important decision: whether or not to forgive the person who has hurt you. God's instructions are clear: He wants you to forgive. Period.

SOMETHING TO REMEMBER

Today, think about the people (including yourself) whom you still need to forgive. And then ask God to help you forgive them. Remember that when you forgive, you're giving yourself a gift. And, remember that God doesn't say that forgiveness is optional; it's a commandment.

MORE FROM GOD'S WORD ABOUT FORGIVENESS

Be even-tempered, content with second place, quick to forgive an offense. Forgive as quickly and completely as the Master forgave you. And regardless of what else you put on, wear love. It's your basic, all-purpose garment. Never be without it.

Colossians 3:13-14 MSG

Be kind to one another, tender-hearted, forgiving each other, just as God in Christ also has forgiven you.

Ephesians 4:32 NASB

And forgive us our sins, for we ourselves also forgive everyone in debt to us. And do not bring us into temptation.

Luke 11:4 NKJV

Our Father is kind; you be kind. Don't pick on people, jump on their failures, criticize their faults—unless, of course, you want the same treatment. Don't condemn those who are down; that hardness can boomerang. Be easy on people; you'll find life a lot easier.

Luke 6:36-37 MSG

MORE POWERFUL IDEAS ABOUT FORGIVENESS

Only the truly forgiven are truly forgiving.

C. S. Lewis

Our relationships with other people are of primary importance to God. Because God is love, He cannot tolerate any unforgiveness or hardness in us toward any individual.

Catherine Marshall

Forgiveness is not an emotion. Forgiveness is an act of the will, and the will can function regardless of the temperature of the heart.

Corrie ten Boom

Revenge is the raging fire that consumes the arsonist.

Max Lucado

The more you practice the art of forgiving, the quicker you'll master the art of living.

Marie T. Freeman

Our forgiveness toward others should flow from a realization and appreciation of God's forgiveness toward us.

Franklin Graham

QUESTIONS TO CONSIDER

Am I willing to acknowledge the important role that forgiveness should play in my life?

_____

_____

Will I strive to forgive those who have hurt me, even when doing so is difficult?

_____

_____

Do I understand that forgiveness is a marathon (not a sprint), and will I prayerfully ask God to help me move beyond the emotions of bitterness and regret?

_____

_____

A PRAYER FOR TODAY

Heavenly Father, forgiveness is Your commandment, and I know that I should forgive others just as You have forgiven me. But, genuine forgiveness is difficult. Help me to forgive those who have injured me, and deliver me from the traps of anger and bitterness. Forgiveness is Your way, Lord; let it be mine. Amen

Day 17

THE THINGS YOU CANNOT CHANGE

I have learned to be content in whatever circumstances I am.
Philippians 4:11 HCSB

THE FOCUS FOR TODAY

People, places, and things were never meant
to give us life. God alone is the author of a fulfilling life.
Gary Smalley & John Trent

The American theologian Reinhold Niebuhr composed a profoundly simple verse that came to be known as the Serenity Prayer: "God, grant me the serenity to accept the things I cannot change, the courage to change the things I can, and the wisdom to know the difference." Niebuhr's words are far easier to recite than they are to live by. Why? Because most of us want life to unfold in accordance with our own wishes and timetables. But sometimes God has other plans.

Author Hannah Whitall Smith observed, "How changed our lives would be if we could only fly through the days on wings of surrender and trust!" These words remind us that even when we cannot understand the workings of God, we must trust Him and accept His will.

So if you've encountered unfortunate circumstances that are beyond your power to control, accept those circumstances . . . and trust God. When you do, you can be comforted in the knowledge that your Creator is both loving and wise, and that He understands His plans perfectly, even when you do not.

ACCEPTING THE UNCHANGEABLE PAST

Has disappointment or tragedy left you feeling embittered toward God and angry at the world? If so, it's time to accept the unchangeable past and to have faith in the promise of tomorrow. It's time to trust God completely—and it's time to reclaim the peace, His peace—that can and should be yours.

God doesn't explain Himself in ways that we, as mortals with limited insight and clouded vision, can comprehend. So, instead of understanding every aspect of God's unfolding plan for our lives and our universe, we must be satisfied to trust Him completely. We cannot know God's motivations, nor can we understand His actions. We can, however, trust Him, and we must.

SOMETHING TO REMEMBER

When you encounter tragic situations that you cannot change, you must learn to trust God and entrust the past to His hands.

MORE FROM GOD'S WORD ABOUT ACCEPTANCE

He is the Lord. Let him do what he thinks is best.

1 Samuel 3:18 NCV

Give in to God, come to terms with him and everything will turn out just fine.

Job 22:21 MSG

A man's heart plans his way, but the Lord determines his steps.

Proverbs 16:9 HCSB

For everything created by God is good, and nothing should be rejected if it is received with thanksgiving.

1 Timothy 4:4 HCSB

Sheathe your sword! Should I not drink the cup that the Father has given Me?

John 18:11 HCSB

MORE FROM GOD'S WORD ABOUT BITTERNESS

All bitterness, anger and wrath, insult and slander must be removed from you, along with all wickedness. And be kind and compassionate to one another, forgiving one another, just as God also forgave you in Christ.

Ephesians 4:31-32 HCSB

But now you must also put away all the following: anger, wrath, malice, slander, and filthy language from your mouth.

Colossians 3:8 HCSB

But if you harbor bitter envy and selfish ambition in your hearts, do not boast about it or deny the truth. Such "wisdom" does not come down from heaven but is earthly, unspiritual, of the devil. For where you have envy and selfish ambition, there you find disorder and every evil practice.

James 3:14-16 NIV

The Lord says, "Forget what happened before, and do not think about the past. Look at the new thing I am going to do. It is already happening. Don't you see it? I will make a road in the desert and rivers in the dry land."

Isaiah 43:18-19 NCV

MORE POWERFUL IDEAS ABOUT ACCEPTANCE

We cannot always understand the ways of Almighty God—the crosses which he sends us, the sacrifices which he demands of us. But, if we accept with faith and resignation his holy will—with no looking back to what might have been—we are at peace.

Rose Fitzgerald Kennedy

If we were given all we wanted here, our hearts would settle for this world rather than the next.

Elisabeth Elliot

The only way you can experience abundant life is to surrender your plans to Him.

Charles Stanley

It would be wrong to have a "poverty complex," for to think ourselves paupers is to deny either the King's riches or to deny our being His children.

Catherine Marshall

Instead of living a black-and-white existence, we'll be released into a Technicolor world of vibrancy and emotion when we more accurately reflect His nature to the world around us.

Bill Hybels

MORE POWERFUL IDEAS ABOUT BITTERNESS

Bitterness only makes suffering worse and closes the spiritual channels through which God can pour His grace.

Warren Wiersbe

Grudges are like hand grenades; It is wise to release them before they destroy you.

Barbara Johnson

Bitterness is a spiritual cancer, a rapidly growing malignancy that can consume your life. Bitterness cannot be ignored but must be healed at the very core, and only Christ can heal bitterness.

Beth Moore

Forgiveness is the key that unlocks the door of resentment and the handcuffs of hate. It is a power that breaks the chains of bitterness and the shackles of selfishness.

Corrie ten Boom

By not forgiving, by not letting wrongs go, we aren't getting back at anyone. We are merely punishing ourselves by barricading our own hearts.

Jim Cymbala

QUESTIONS TO CONSIDER

Am I genuinely trying to accept the past, even when the past is painful?

_____

_____

Do I believe that it is important to trust God even when I don't understand why certain things happen?

_____

_____

Am I willing to change the things I can change and accept the things I can't?

_____

_____

A PRAYER FOR TODAY
_Father, the events of this world unfold according
to a plan that I cannot fully understand. But You
understand. Help me to trust You, Lord, even when
I am grieving. Help me to trust You even when I am
confused. Today, in whatever circumstances
I find myself, let me trust Your will and accept
Your love . . . completely. Amen_

Day 18

KEEP PRAYING!

Is anyone among you suffering?
He should pray.
James 5:13 HCSB

THE FOCUS FOR TODAY

It was the darkest hour of my life; relief came in prayer.
God heard my cry, and enabled me to say,
from the depth of my soul, "Thy will be done."

Dwight L Moody

Living with intense grief is a marathon, not a sprint—it is a journey that unfolds day by day. And, that's exactly how often you should seek direction from your Creator: one day at a time, each day followed by the next, without exception.

Daily prayer and meditation is a matter of will and habit. You must willingly organize your time by carving out quiet moments with God, and you must form the habit of daily worship. When you do, you'll discover that no time is more precious than the silent moments you spend with your Heavenly Father.

The quality of your spiritual life will be in direct proportion to the quality of your prayer life. Prayer changes things, and it changes you. So today, instead of turning things over in your mind, turn them over to God in prayer. Instead of worrying about your next decision, ask God to lead the way. Don't limit your prayers to meals or to bedtime; pray constantly. God is listening; He wants to hear from you; and you most certainly need to hear from Him.

LISTEN CAREFULLY

Can you quiet yourself long enough to listen to your conscience? Are you attuned to the subtle guidance of your intuition? Are you willing to pray sincerely and then to wait quietly for God's response. Hopefully so.

Sometimes God speaks loudly and clearly. More often, He speaks in a quiet voice—and if you are wise, you will be listening carefully when He does. To do so, you must carve out quiet moments each day to study His Word and sense His direction.

Usually God refrains from sending His messages on stone tablets or city billboards. More often, He communicates in subtler ways. If you sincerely desire to hear His voice, you must listen carefully, and you must do so in the silent corners of your quiet, willing heart.

SOMETHING TO REMEMBER

Sometimes, the answer is "No." God does not answer all of our prayers in the affirmative, nor should He. His job is not to grant all our earthly requests; His job is to offer us eternal salvation (for which we must be eternally grateful). When we are disappointed by the realities of life-here-on-earth, we should remember that our prayers are always answered by a sovereign, all-knowing God, and that we must trust Him, whether He answers "Yes," "No," or "Not yet."

MORE FROM GOD'S WORD ABOUT PRAYER

Rejoice always, pray without ceasing, in everything give thanks; for this is the will of God in Christ Jesus for you.

1 Thessalonians 5:16-18 NKJV

Whatever you ask for in prayer, believe that you have received it, and it will be yours.

Mark 11:24 NIV

I sought the LORD, and he heard me, and delivered me from all my fears.

Psalm 34:4 KJV

Ask and it shall be given to you; seek and you shall find; knock and it shall be opened to you. For every one who asks receives, and he who seeks finds, and to him who knocks it shall be opened.

Matthew 7:7-8 NASB

Rejoice in hope; be patient in affliction; be persistent in prayer.

Romans 12:12 HCSB

MORE POWERFUL IDEAS ABOUT PRAYER

To pray much is to knock for Him to Whom we pray. This is often done more by groans than speeches, by weeping than by addresses.

St. Augustine

As we join together in prayer, we draw on God's enabling might in a way that multiplies our own efforts many times over.

Shirley Dobson

The center of power is not to be found in summit meetings or in peace conferences. It is not in Peking or Washington or the United Nations, but rather where a child of God prays in the power of the Spirit for God's will to be done in her life, in her home, and in the world around her.

Ruth Bell Graham

We must leave it to God to answer our prayers in His own wisest way. Sometimes, we are so impatient and think that God does not answer. God always answers! He never fails! Be still. Abide in Him.

Mrs. Charles E. Cowman

When you ask God to do
something, don't ask timidly;
put your whole heart into it.

—

Marie T. Freeman

When any needy heart begins to truly pray, heaven itself stirs in response.

Jim Cymbala

When there is a matter that requires definite prayer, pray until you believe God and until you can thank Him for His answer.

Hannah Whitall Smith

We have to pray with our eyes on God, not on the difficulties.

Oswald Chambers

Storm the throne of grace and persevere therein, and mercy will come down.

John Wesley

Prayer succeeds when all else fails.

E. M. Bounds

Pray, and let God worry.

Martin Luther

QUESTIONS TO CONSIDER

Do I understand that prayer strengthens my relationship with God?

_____

_____

Do I trust that God will care for me, even when it seems that my prayers have gone unanswered?

_____

_____

Do I believe that my prayers have the power to change my circumstances calm my fears, and lessen my pain?

_____

_____

A PRAYER FOR TODAY

Dear Lord, when I open my heart to You, You respond to me. I will take my fears, my sorrows, and my hopes to You in prayer. And, then, I will trust the answers that You give, today and every day that I live. Amen

Day 19

ALWAYS HOPE

Hope deferred makes the heart sick.
Proverbs 13:12 NKJV

THE FOCUS FOR TODAY

Tears are permitted to us, but they must glisten
in the light of faith and hope.
C. H. Spurgeon

On the darkest days of our lives, we may be confronted with an illusion that seems very real indeed: the illusion of hopelessness. Try though we might, we simply can't envision a solution to our problems—and we fall into the darkness of despair. During these times, we may question God—His love, His presence, even His very existence. Despite God's promises, despite Christ's love, and despite our many blessings, we may envision little or no hope for the future. These dark days can be dangerous times for us and for our loved ones.

If you find yourself falling into the spiritual traps of worry and discouragement, seek the encouraging words of fellow Christians, and the healing touch of Jesus. After all, it was Christ who promised, "These things I have spoken unto you, that in me ye might have peace. In the world ye shall have tribulation: but be of good cheer; I have overcome the world" (John 16:33 KJV).

Can you place your future into the hands of a loving and all-knowing God? Can you live amid the uncertainties of today, knowing that God has dominion over all your tomorrows? Can you summon the faith to trust God in good times and hard times? If you can, you are wise and you are blessed.

HOPE RENEWED

Sometimes, hope can be a highly perishable commodity. When the challenges and sorrows of everyday life threaten to overwhelm us, we may convince ourselves that the future holds little promise—and we may allow our fears to eclipse our dreams.

When hope seems to be in short supply, there is a source to which we can turn in order to restore our perspective and our strength. That source is God. When we lift our prayers to the Creator, we avail ourselves of God's power, God's wisdom, and God's love. And when we allow God's Son to reign over our hearts, we are transformed, not just for a day, but for all eternity.

Are you looking for a renewed sense of hope? If so, it's time to place your future in the loving hands of God's only begotten Son. When you do, you'll discover that hope is not only highly perishable, but that it is also readily renewable . . . one day—and one moment—at a time.

SOMETHING TO REMEMBER

If you're experiencing hard times, you'll be wise to start spending more time with God. And if you do your part, God will do His part. So never be afraid to hope—or to ask—for a miracle.

MORE FROM GOD'S WORD ABOUT HOPE

Let us hold on to the confession of our hope without wavering, for He who promised is faithful.

Hebrews 10:23 HCSB

For I hope in You, O LORD; You will answer, O Lord my God.

Psalm 38:15 NASB

The Lord is good to those whose hope is in him, to the one who seeks him; it is good to wait quietly for the salvation of the Lord.

Lamentations 3:25-26 NIV

May the God of hope fill you with all joy and peace as you trust in him, so that you may overflow with hope by the power of the Holy Spirit.

Romans 15:13 NIV

Now faith is the substance of things hoped for, the evidence of things not seen.

Hebrews 11:1 KJV

MORE POWERFUL IDEAS ABOUT HOPE

Oh, remember this: There is never a time when we may not hope in God. Whatever our necessities, however great our difficulties, and though to all appearance, help is impossible, yet our business is to hope in God, and it will be found that it is not in vain.

George Mueller

We must face today as children of tomorrow. We must meet the uncertainties of this world with the certainty of the world to come. To the pure in heart nothing really bad can happen . . . not death, but sin, should be our greatest fear.

A. W. Tozer

I wish I could make it all new again; I can't. But God can. "He restores my soul," wrote the shepherd. God doesn't reform; he restores. He doesn't camouflage the old; he restores the new. The Master Builder will pull out the original plan and restore it. He will restore the vigor; he will restore the energy. He will restore the hope. He will restore the soul.

Max Lucado

QUESTIONS TO CONSIDER

Do I believe that genuine hope begins with hope in a sovereign God?

_____

_____

Am I confident in God's promise to protect me now and throughout all eternity?

_____

_____

Do I really believe that God offers me "a peace that passes understanding," and do I really desire to accept God's peace?

_____

_____

A PRAYER FOR TODAY

Lord, when my heart is troubled, let me trust in You. When I lose faith in this world, let me hold tightly to my faith in You. Remind me, Dear Lord, that in every situation and in every season of life, You will love me and protect me. You are my strength, Father, and I need never lose hope because You remain sovereign today and forever. Amen

Day 20

WORSHIP HIM

*God is Spirit, and those who worship Him
must worship in spirit and truth.*
John 4:24 HCSB

THE FOCUS FOR TODAY

When your grief presses you to the very dust,
worship there.

C. H. Spurgeon

While you're working through the grieving process, worship—when, where, and how you worship—can have a profound impact on your recovery. If you worship God sincerely and often, you'll be blessed by the time you spend with the Creator. But if your pain causes you to withdraw from your church, or from God, you'll be doing yourself a severe disservice.

If you're enduring difficult times (or if you're not), be sure to worship God seven days a week, not just on Sundays. Start each day with a time of prayer and Bible study. Then, throughout the day, talk to God often. When you do, He will strengthen your spirit and guide your steps.

So as you move through and beyond your grief, make worship a cornerstone of your recovery. Let God's transcendent love surround you and transform you, today and every day.

WORSHIP HIM EVERY DAY

Do you take time each day to worship your Father in heaven, or do you wait until Sunday morning to praise Him for His blessings? The answer to this question will, in large part, determine the quality and direction of your spiritual life.

When we worship God every day of our lives, we are blessed. When we fail to worship God, for whatever reason, we forfeit the spiritual gifts that He intends for us.

Every day provides opportunities to put God where He belongs: at the center of our lives. When we do so, we worship Him not only with our words, but also with our deeds, and that's as it should be. For believers, God comes first. Always first.

SOMETHING TO REMEMBER

Worship reminds you of an important truth: God understands your grief, and He can heal your heart. So worship Him every day; no exceptions.

MORE FROM GOD'S WORD ABOUT WORSHIP

If anyone is thirsty, he should come to Me and drink!

John 7:37 HCSB

Worship the Lord your God and . . . serve Him only.

Matthew 4:10 HCSB

So that at the name of Jesus every knee should bow—of those who are in heaven and on earth and under the earth—and every tongue should confess that Jesus Christ is Lord, to the glory of God the Father.

Philippians 2:10-11 HCSB

I rejoiced with those who said to me, "Let us go to the house of the Lord."

Psalm 122:1 HCSB

And every day they devoted themselves to meeting together in the temple complex, and broke bread from house to house. They ate their food with gladness and simplicity of heart, praising God and having favor with all the people. And every day the Lord added those being saved to them.

Acts 2:46-47 HCSB

More Powerful Ideas About Worship

It's the definition of worship: A hungry heart finding the Father's feast. A searching soul finding the Father's face. A wandering pilgrim spotting the Father's house. Finding God. Finding God seeking us. This is worship. This is a worshiper.

Max Lucado

In Biblical worship you do not find the repetition of a phrase; instead, you find the worshipers rehearsing the character of God and His ways, reminding Him of His faithfulness and His wonderful promises.

Kay Arthur

We worship God not because He will make our path smooth, but because He gives us the grace and determination to keep walking even when the path is rocky.

Harold Kushner

Worship is God-centered, aware of one another only in that deep, joyous awareness of being caught up together in God.

Anne Ortlund

Worship is your spirit responding to God's Spirit.

Rick Warren

QUESTIONS TO CONSIDER

Do I believe that it is important to worship God every day of the week, not just on Sundays?

_____

_____

Do I feel that it is important to worship regularly with the community of believers?

_____

_____

Do I have a quiet place where I can go, a place where God seems especially close?

_____

_____

A PRAYER FOR TODAY

*When I worship You, Dear Lord, You set my path—
and my heart—straight. Let this day and every day be a
time of worship. Whether I am in Your house or simply
going about my daily activities, let me worship You,
not only with words and deeds, but also with my heart.
In the quiet moments of the day, I will praise You for
loving me, guiding me, and saving me. Amen*

Day 21

BEYOND WORRY

For God has not given us a spirit of fearfulness,
but one of power, love, and sound judgment.
2 Timothy 1:7 HCSB

THE FOCUS FOR TODAY

We need to understand that at the time of intense pain
brought about by the loss of a loved one,
it is natural for little seeds of doubt about our faith
to creep into our minds and hearts.
Zig Ziglar

Because we are imperfect human beings living imperfect lives, we worry. Even though we, as Christians, have the assurance of salvation—even though we, as believers, have the promise of God's love and protection—we find ourselves fretting over the countless details of everyday life. Jesus understood our concerns, and He addressed them.

In the 6th chapter of Matthew, Jesus makes it clear that the heart of God is a protective, caring heart:

Therefore I say to you, do not worry about your life, what you will eat or what you will drink; nor about your body, what you will put on. Is not life more than food and the body more than clothing? Look at the birds of the air, for they neither sow nor reap nor gather into barns; yet your heavenly Father feeds them. Are you not of more value than they? Which of you by worrying can add one cubit to his stature? . . . Therefore do not worry about tomorrow, for tomorrow will worry about its own things. Sufficient for the day is its own trouble. (vv. 25-27, 34 KJV)

Perhaps you're worried about your future or your health or your finances or any of a hundred other things. If so, make Matthew 6 a regular part of your daily Bible reading. This beautiful passage will remind you that God still sits in His heaven and you are His beloved child. Then, perhaps, you will worry a little less and trust God a little more, and that's as it should be because God is trustworthy . . . and you are protected.

GOD CAN HANDLE IT

It's a promise that is made over and over again in the Bible: Whatever "it" is, God can handle it.

Life isn't always easy. Far from it! Sometimes, life can be very, very difficult, indeed. But even when the storm clouds form overhead, even during our darkest moments, we're protected by a loving Heavenly Father.

When we're worried, God can reassure us; when we're sad, God can comfort us. When our hearts are broken, God is not just near; He is here. So we must lift our thoughts and prayers to Him. When we do, He will answer our prayers. Why? Because He is our Shepherd, and He has promised to protect us now and forever.

SOMETHING TO REMEMBER

If you're feeling discouraged or despondent, try to redirect your thoughts away from your losses—focus, instead, upon God's love, God's blessings, and God's plan for your life. And while you're at it, remember that the grief you feel today will lessen over time. So be patient and be hopeful.

MORE FROM GOD'S WORD ABOUT
THE NEED FOR OPTIMISM

The Lord is my light and my salvation; whom shall I fear? The Lord is the strength of my life; of whom shall I be afraid?

Psalm 27:1 KJV

Make me to hear joy and gladness . . . .

Psalm 51:8 KJV

I can do everything through him that gives me strength.

Philippians 4:13 NIV

Be of good courage, and he shall strengthen your heart, all ye that hope in the LORD.

Psalm 31:24 KJV

Finally, brethren, whatsoever things are true, whatsoever things are honest, whatsoever things are just, whatsoever things are pure, whatsoever things are lovely, whatsoever things are of good report; if there be any virtue, and if there be any praise, think on these things.

Philippians 4:8 KJV

More Powerful Ideas About Optimism

The people whom I have seen succeed best in life have always been cheerful and hopeful people who went about their business with a smile on their faces.

Charles Kingsley

If you can't tell whether your glass is half-empty or half-full, you don't need another glass; what you need is better eyesight . . . and a more thankful heart.

Marie T. Freeman

The game was to just find something about everything to be glad about—no matter what it was. You see, when you're hunting for the glad things, you sort of forget the other kind.

Eleanor H. Porter

Dark as my path may seem to others, I carry a magic light in my heart. Faith, the spiritual strong searchlight, illumines the way, and although sinister doubts lurk in the shadow, I walk unafraid toward the enchanted wood where the foliage is always green, where joy abides, where nightingales nest and sing, and where life and death are one in the presence of the Lord.

Helen Keller

QUESTIONS TO CONSIDER

Even when I'm hurting, do I try to count my blessings?

_____

_____

Do I spend time with people who encourage me to focus on God's love, God's blessings, and God's Son?

_____

_____

Even when I can't understand why bad things happen, am I willing to trust God and to seek His will for my life?

_____

_____

A PRAYER FOR TODAY
Thank You, Lord, for Your infinite love.
Make me an optimistic Christian, Father,
as I place my hope and my trust in You. Amen

Day 22

GOD'S PROTECTION

Though I sit in darkness, the Lord will be my light.
Micah 7:8 HCSB

THE FOCUS FOR TODAY

By ourselves we are not capable of suffering bravely,
but the Lord possesses all the strength we lack
and will demonstrate His power when
we undergo persecution.

Corrie ten Boom

God is our greatest refuge. When every earthly support system fails, God remains steadfast, and His love remains unchanged. When we encounter life's inevitable disappointments and setbacks, God remains faithful. When we suffer losses that leave us breathless, God is always with for us, always ready to respond to our prayers, always working in us and through us to turn tragedy into triumph.

God's hand uplifts those who turn their hearts and prayers to Him. Count yourself among that number. When you do, you can live courageously, knowing that "this too will pass"—but that God's love for you will not. And you can draw strength from the knowledge that you are a marvelous creation, loved, protected, and uplifted by the ever-present hand of God.

TRUST GOD'S PROMISES

God has made quite a few promises to you, and He will keep every single one of them. Elisabeth Elliot observed, "We have ample evidence that the Lord is able to guide. The promises cover every imaginable situation. All we need to do is to take the hand he stretches out." And her words apply to you and to every situation you will ever encounter.

Have you endured a painful loss? The Bible promises that God can ease your pain. Are you fearful, anxious, fretful, or troubled? God promises that He will protect you, now and throughout eternity. Has your world been turned upside down? God promises that He is sufficient to meet your every need.

Whatever dangers you may face, whatever heartbreaks you must endure, God is with you, and He stands ready to protect you.

The Psalmist writes, "Weeping may endure for a night, but joy comes in the morning" (Psalm 30:5 NKJV). But when we are suffering, the morning may seem very far away. It is not. God promises that He is "near to those who have a broken heart" (Psalm 34:18 NKJV). So you can live victoriously, knowing that even in times of suffering, God is as near as your next breath—and you are always protected.

SOMETHING TO REMEMBER

Grief is a universal fact of life; no man or woman, no matter how righteous, is exempt. Christians, however, face their grief with the ultimate armor: God's promises. God will help heal us if we let Him into our hearts. And the time to let Him in is now.

MORE FROM GOD'S WORD ABOUT
GOD'S PROTECTION

Finally, my brethren, be strong in the Lord and in the power of His might. Put on the whole armor of God, that you may be able to stand against the wiles of the devil.

Ephesians 6:10-11 NKJV

The Lord your God in your midst, The Mighty One, will save; He will rejoice over you with gladness, He will quiet you with His love, He will rejoice over you with singing.

Zephaniah 3:17 NKJV

God is my shield, saving those whose hearts are true and right.

Psalm 7:10 NLT

Those who trust the Lord are like Mount Zion, which sits unmoved forever. As the mountains surround Jerusalem, the Lord surrounds his people now and forever.

Psalm 125:1-2 NCV

But the Lord will be a refuge for His people.

Joel 3:16 HCSB

MORE POWERFUL IDEAS ABOUT GOD'S PROTECTION

The grace of God runs downhill toward the ones who are emptied and vulnerable, toward the ones who admit that they struggle.

Angela Thomas

God gives His gifts where He finds the vessel empty enough to receive them.

C. S. Lewis

We are not called to be burden-bearers, but cross-bearers and light-bearers. We must cast our burdens on the Lord.

Corrie ten Boom

Our tears do not fall without the hand of God catching every one.

Kathy Troccoli

Deep in the dark night of the suffering soul comes a moment when nothing intellectual or psychological matters. It is the time of the touch, the tender touch, a hand held, a cheek kissed, a holy embrace that conveys more to the human spirit than anything from tongue or pen.

Bill Bright

We can take great comfort
that God never sleeps—
so we can.

—

Dianna Booher

In all the old castles of England, there was a place called the keep. It was always the strongest and best protected place in the castle, and in it were hidden all who were weak and helpless and unable to defend themselves in times of danger. Shall we be afraid to hide ourselves in the keeping power of our Divine Keeper, who neither slumbers nor sleeps, and who has promised to preserve our going out and our coming in, from this time forth and even forever more?

Hannah Whitall Smith

Trials are medicines which our gracious and wise physician prescribes because we need them; and he proportions the frequency and weight of them to what the case requires. Let us trust in his skill and thank him for his prescription.

John Newton

It has been the faith of the Son of God who loves me and gave Himself for me that has held me in the darkest valley and the hottest fires and the deepest waters.

Elisabeth Elliot

Trouble is one of God's great servants because it reminds us how much we continually need the Lord.

Jim Cymbala

QUESTIONS TO CONSIDER

Do I believe that God will protect my family now and throughout eternity?

_____

_____

Do I trust God's plans even when I cannot understand them?

_____

_____

Am I willing to accept God's unfolding plan for the world—and for my world?

_____

_____

A PRAYER FOR TODAY

Lord, sometimes life is difficult. And sometimes,
I am worried, weary, or heartbroken. But, when I lift
my eyes to You, Father, You strengthen me.
When I am weak, You lift me up. Today, I will turn
to You for strength, for hope, for direction,
and for deliverance. Amen

Day 23

GRIEF AND GROWTH

Wisdom is a tree of life to those who embrace her;
happy are those who hold her tightly.

Proverbs 3:18 NLT

THE FOCUS FOR TODAY

Since adversity is God's most effective tool insofar as
spiritual growth is concerned, the degree to which we
desire to grow spiritually corresponds to our ability to
handle adversity successfully.

Charles Stanley

The path to spiritual maturity unfolds day by day, through good times and bad. Each day offers the opportunity to worship God, to ignore God, or to rebel against God. When we worship Him with our prayers, our words, our thoughts, and our actions, we are blessed by the richness of our relationship with the Father. But if we ignore God altogether or intentionally rebel against His commandments, we rob ourselves of His blessings.

Many of life's most important lessons are painful to learn, so times of grief can also be times of growth. But spiritual growth need not take place only in times of suffering. We must seek to grow in our knowledge and love of the Lord in every season of life. Thankfully, God always stands at the door; whenever we are ready to reach out to Him, He will answer.

Has your heart been broken? Or are you enduring tough times that have left your head spinning? If so, you can be certain that God still has important lessons to teach you. So ask yourself this: What lesson is God trying to teach me today? And then go about the business of learning it.

TO GROW SPIRITUALLY, YOU MUST FORGIVE

Forgiveness is an exercise in spiritual growth: the more we forgive, the more we grow. Conversely, bitterness makes spiritual growth impossible: when our hearts are filled with resentment and anger, there is no room left for love.

As Christians, we can and should continue to grow in the love and the knowledge of our Savior as long as we live. When we cease to grow, either emotionally or spiritually, we do ourselves and our loved ones a profound disservice. But, if we study God's Word, if we obey His commandments, and if we live in the center of His will, we will not be "stagnant" believers; we will, instead, be growing Christians . . . and that's exactly what God wants for our lives.

In those quiet moments when we open our hearts to God, the Creator who made us keeps remaking us. He gives us direction, perspective, wisdom, and courage. And the appropriate moment to accept His spiritual gifts is always this one.

SOMETHING TO REMEMBER

The times that test our souls can also be times of intense personal growth. Elisabeth Elliot observed, "I am not a theologian or a scholar, but I am very aware of the fact that pain is necessary to all of us. In my own life, I think I can honestly say that out of the deepest pain has come the strongest conviction of the presence of God and the love of God."

MORE FROM GOD'S WORD ABOUT
SPIRITUAL GROWTH

For this reason also, since the day we heard this, we haven't stopped praying for you. We are asking that you may be filled with the knowledge of His will in all wisdom and spiritual understanding.

Colossians 1:9 HCSB

I want their hearts to be encouraged and joined together in love, so that they may have all the riches of assured understanding, and have the knowledge of God's mystery—Christ.

Colossians 2:2 HCSB

MORE POWERFUL IDEAS ABOUT SPIRITUAL GROWTH

Our vision is so limited we can hardly imagine a love that does not show itself in protection from suffering. The love of God did not protect His own Son. He will not necessarily protect us—not from anything it takes to make us like His Son. A lot of hammering and chiseling and purifying by fire will have to go into the process.

Elisabeth Elliot

In the soul-searching of our lives, we are to stay quiet so we can hear Him say all that He wants to say to us in our hearts.

Charles Swindoll

Grief drives men into the habits of serious reflection, sharpens the understanding, and softens the heart.

John Adams

God the Father has allowed my body to be struck in the physical sense, but the striking has only set off a spiritual vibration, and the tone and pitch of it are of heaven in my soul.

Bill Bright

QUESTIONS TO CONSIDER

Do I believe that God still has lessons to teach me?

_____

_____

Do I believe that I still have "room to grow" in my faith?

_____

_____

Do I believe that spiritual growth usually happens day by day, and do I try to keep growing every day?

_____

_____

A PRAYER FOR TODAY

Lord, when I feel overwhelmed with sadness,
I will turn to You. Help me to live according to
Your Word, Father, and let me grow in my faith
every day that I live. Amen

Day 24

FINALLY MAKING PEACE WITH THE PAST

Peace I leave with you, my peace I give unto you:
not as the world giveth, give I unto you.
Let not your heart be troubled, neither let it be afraid.

John 14:27 KJV

THE FOCUS FOR TODAY

The better acquainted you become with God,
the less tension you feel and the more peace you possess.

Charles Allen

Some of life's greatest roadblocks are not the ones we see through the windshield; they are, instead, the roadblocks that seem to fill the rearview mirror. Because we are imperfect human beings who lack perfect control over our thoughts, we may allow ourselves to become "stuck" in the past—even though we know better. Instead of focusing our thoughts and energies on the opportunities of today, we may allow painful memories to fill our minds and sap our strength. We simply can't seem to let go of our pain, so we relive it again and again . . . with predictably unfortunate consequences. Thankfully, God has other plans.

Philippians 3:13-14 instructs us to focus on the future, not the past: "One thing I do, forgetting those things which are behind and reaching forward to those things which are ahead, I press toward the goal for the prize of the upward call of God in Christ Jesus" (NKJV). Yet for many of us, focusing on the future is difficult indeed. Why? Part of the problem has to do with forgiveness. When we find ourselves focusing too intently on the past, it's a sure sign that we need to focus, instead, on a more urgent need: the need to forgive. Until we thoroughly and completely forgive those who have hurt us—and until we completely forgive ourselves—we remain stuck. Yet focusing too intently on the past is, almost without exception, futile. No amount of anger or bitterness can change what happened yesterday. Tears can't change the past; regrets can't change it. Our worries won't change the past, and neither will our complaints. Simply put, the past is, and always will be, the past. Forever.

Can you summon both the courage and the wisdom to accept your past and move on with your life? Can you accept the reality that yesterday—and all the yesterdays before it—are gone? And, can you entrust all those yesterdays to God? Hopefully you can.

Once you have made peace with your past, you are free to become fully engaged in the present. And when you become fully engaged in the present, you are then free to build a better future for yourself and your loved ones.

If you've endured a difficult past, learn from it, mourn it, memorialize it if you must, but don't live in it. Instead, build your future on a firm foundation of trust and forgiveness: trust in your Heavenly Father, and forgiveness for all His children, including yourself. Give all your yesterdays to God, and celebrate this day with hope in your heart and praise on your lips. Your Creator intends to use you in wonderful, unexpected ways if you let Him. But first, God wants you to make peace with your past . . . and He wants you to do it now.

SOMETHING TO REMEMBER

Does peace seem to be a distant promise? It is not.
God's peace is available to you this very moment if
you place absolute trust in Him.

MORE FROM GOD'S WORD ABOUT PEACE

God has called us to live in peace.

1 Corinthians 7:15 NIV

*And let the peace of God rule in your hearts . . . and be ye
thankful.*

Colossians 3:15 KJV

*You will keep in perfect peace him whose mind is steadfast,
because he trusts in you.*

Isaiah 26:3 NIV

*I have told you these things, so that in me you may have peace.
In this world you will have trouble. But take heart! I have
overcome the world.*

John 16:33 NIV

MORE POWERFUL IDEAS ABOUT PEACE

A great many people are trying to make peace, but that has already been done. God has not left it for us to do; all we have to do is to enter into it.

D. L. Moody

For Jesus peace seems to have meant not the absence of struggle but the presence of love.

Frederick Buechner

The Christian has a deep, silent, hidden peace, which the world sees not, like some well in a retired and shady place.

John Henry Cardinal Newman

That peace, which has been described and which believers enjoy, is a participation of the peace which their glorious Lord and Master himself enjoys.

Jonathan Edwards

Prayer guards hearts and minds and causes God to bring peace out of chaos.

Beth Moore

QUESTIONS TO CONSIDER

Am I able to learn from the past and accept the past, but live in the present?

_____

_____

Do I believe that it is important to trust God even when I don't understand why certain things happen?

_____

_____

Am I willing to change the things I can change and accept the things I can't?

_____

_____

A PRAYER FOR TODAY

_Father, when I turn my thoughts and prayers to You,
I feel Your peace. But sometimes, Lord, I become
distracted by worry or sadness or fear. Turn my
thoughts back to You. You are the Giver of all things
good, and You give me comfort when I draw close to
You. Help me to trust Your will, to follow
Your commands, and to accept Your peace,
today and forever. Amen_

Day 25

TIME FOR RENEWAL

I waited patiently for the Lord; And He inclined to me,
And heard my cry. He also brought me up out of a horrible
pit, Out of the miry clay, And set my feet upon a rock,
And established my steps. He has put a new song in my
mouth—Praise to our God; Many will see it and fear,
And will trust in the Lord.

Psalm 40:1-3 NKJV

THE FOCUS FOR TODAY

He is the God of wholeness and restoration.

Stormie Omartian

In the 40th Psalm, David rejoiced because God had delivered David from sorrow while putting a new song on David's lips. Perhaps you, like David, are enduring the inevitable dark days of life. If so, you must remember that God can renew your spirit, just like He renewed David's.

Even if you're an inspired believer, even if you're normally upbeat about your future and your life, you may, on occasion, find yourself running on empty. Sorrow can drain you of your strength and rob you of the joy that is rightfully yours in Christ.

Are you tired or troubled? Turn your heart toward God in prayer. Are you weak or worried? Take the time—or, more accurately, make the time—to delve deeply into God's Holy Word. Are you spiritually depleted? Call upon fellow believers to support you, and call upon Christ to renew your spirit and your life. When you do, you'll discover that, in time, the Creator of the universe will deliver you from sorrow and place a new song on your lips.

HE RESTORES YOUR SOUL

On occasion, the demands of daily life can drain us of our strength and rob us of the joy that is rightfully ours in Christ. When we find ourselves tired, discouraged, or worse, there is a source from which we can draw the power needed to recharge our spiritual batteries. That source is God.

Is your spiritual battery running low? Is your energy on the wane? Are your emotions frayed? If so, it's time to turn your thoughts and your prayers to your Heavenly Father. When you do, He will provide for your needs, and He will restore your soul.

SOMETHING TO REMEMBER

When you are weak or worried, God can renew your spirit. It's up to you to talk with Him, to listen to Him, and to trust Him completely. When you do these things, you'll discover that God has the power to repair your heart and transform your life.

MORE FROM GOD'S WORD ABOUT RENEWAL

The One who was sitting on the throne said, "Look! I am making everything new!" Then he said, "Write this, because these words are true and can be trusted."

Revelation 21:5 NCV

When doubts filled my mind, your comfort gave me renewed hope and cheer.

Psalm 94:19 NLT

I will give you a new heart and put a new spirit within you.

Ezekiel 36:26 HCSB

But may the God of all grace, who called us to His eternal glory by Christ Jesus, after you have suffered a while, perfect, establish, strengthen, and settle you.

1 Peter 5:10 NKJV

Finally, brothers, rejoice. Be restored, be encouraged, be of the same mind, be at peace, and the God of love and peace will be with you.

2 Corinthians 13:11 HCSB

MORE FROM GOD'S WORD ABOUT JOY

These things I have spoken to you, that My joy may remain in you, and that your joy may be full.

John 15:11 NKJV

A joyful heart is good medicine, but a broken spirit dries up the bones.

Proverbs 17:22 NASB

Always be full of joy in the Lord. I say it again—rejoice!

Philippians 4:4 NLT

Rejoice, and be exceeding glad: for great is your reward in heaven . . . .

Matthew 5:12 KJV

Shout for joy to the LORD, all the earth. Worship the LORD with gladness; come before him with joyful songs.

Psalm 100:1-2 NIV

MORE POWERFUL IDEAS ABOUT RENEWAL

In those desperate times when we feel like we don't have an ounce of strength, He will gently pick up our heads so that our eyes can behold something—something that will keep His hope alive in us.

Kathy Troccoli

No matter how heavy the burden, daily strength is given, so I expect we need not give ourselves any concern as to what the outcome will be. We must simply go forward.

Annie Armstrong

It is true that we endure trials, but it is also true that we are delivered out of them.

C. H. Spurgeon

Each of us has something broken in our lives: a broken promise, a broken dream, a broken marriage, a broken heart . . . and we must decide how we're going to deal with our brokenness. We can wallow in self-pity or regret, accomplishing nothing and having no fun or joy in our circumstances; or we can determine with our will to take a few risks, get out of our comfort zone, and see what God will do to bring unexpected delight in our time of need.

Luci Swindoll

MORE POWERFUL IDEAS ABOUT JOY

The Christian should be an alleluia from head to foot!

St. Augustine

The Christian lifestyle is not one of legalistic do's and don'ts, but one that is positive, attractive, and joyful.

Vonette Bright

Joy in life is not the absence of sorrow. The fact that Jesus could have joy in the midst of sorrow is proof that we can experience this too.

Warren Wiersbe

Christ is not only a remedy for your weariness and trouble, but he will give you an abundance of the contrary: joy and delight. They who come to Christ do not only come to a resting-place after they have been wandering in a wilderness, but they come to a banqueting-house where they may rest, and where they may feast. They may cease from their former troubles and toils, and they may enter upon a course of delights and spiritual joys.

Jonathan Edwards

What is your focus today? Joy comes when it is Jesus first, others second . . . then you.

Kay Arthur

QUESTIONS TO CONSIDER

Do I believe that God has the power to renew my spirit and heal my heart?

_____

_____

Do I firmly believe that God still has important work for me to do?

_____

_____

If I feel God's call, am I willing to strike out in a new direction?

_____

_____

A PRAYER FOR TODAY

Lord, You are my rock and my strength. When I grow weary, let me turn my thoughts and my prayers to You. When I am discouraged, sad, or fearful, restore my faith in You. Let me always trust in Your promises, Lord, and let me draw strength from those promises . . . and from Your unending love. Amen

Day 26

TIME FOR RECOVERY

He will wipe away every tear from their eyes.
Death will exist no longer; grief, crying, and pain will exist
no longer, because the previous things have passed away.

Revelation 21:4 HCSB

THE FOCUS FOR TODAY

When we reach the end of our strength, wisdom,
and personal resources, we enter into the beginning
of his glorious provisions.

Patsy Clairmont

The Book of Ecclesiastes reminds us that, "To everything there is a season, a time for every purpose under heaven" (3:1 NKJV). And in your own life, there is a time for grief and a time for healing. Even if you are currently gripped by an overwhelming sense of loss, rest assured: Better days are ahead. And the quality of those days depends, in large part, upon the quality of your relationship with your Creator.

When you place your faith, your trust, indeed your life in the hands of Christ Jesus, you'll be amazed at His power to transform your life and heal your heart. When you trust His promises and follow His path, you'll be blessed and you'll be comforted. With Him, all things are possible, and He stands ready to open a world of possibilities to you . . . if you have faith.

If you are grieving today, never lose faith that you may find healing tomorrow. God stands ready to offer His healing hand. So why not take His hand right now?

HE IS SUFFICIENT

Of this you can be certain: God is sufficient to meet your needs. Period.

Does your pain seem overwhelming at times? If so, you must learn to rely not only upon your own resources, but also upon the promises of your Father in heaven. God will hold your hand and walk with you and your family if you let Him. So even if your circumstances are difficult, trust the Father.

God promises that He is "near to those who have a broken heart" (Psalm 34:18 NKJV). When we are troubled, we must turn to Him, and we must encourage our friends and family members to do likewise.

So if you are discouraged by the inevitable demands of life here on earth, be mindful of this fact: the loving heart of God is sufficient to meet any challenge . . . including yours.

SOMETHING TO REMEMBER

The grieving process takes time. God does not promise instantaneous healing, but He does promise healing: "I have heard your prayer, I have seen your tears; surely I will heal you" (2 Kings 20:5 NKJV).

MORE FROM GOD'S WORD ABOUT NEW BEGINNINGS

Create in me a pure heart, O God, and renew a steadfast spirit within me.

Psalm 51:10 NIV

. . . inwardly we are being renewed day by day.

2 Corinthians 4:16 NIV

I will give you a new heart and put a new spirit in you . . . .

Ezekiel 36:26 NIV

Remember ye not the former things, neither consider the things of old. Behold, I will do a new thing . . . .

Isaiah 43:18-19 KJV

When doubts filled my mind, your comfort gave me renewed hope and cheer.

Psalm 94:19 NLT

MORE POWERFUL IDEAS ABOUT NEW BEGINNINGS

Each of us has something broken in our lives: a broken promise, a broken dream, a broken marriage, a broken heart . . . and we must decide how we're going to deal with our brokenness. We can wallow in self-pity or regret, accomplishing nothing and having no fun or joy in our circumstances; or we can determine with our will to take a few risks, get out of our comfort zone, and see what God will do to bring unexpected delight in our time of need.

Luci Swindoll

God specializes in things fresh and firsthand. His plans for you this year may outshine those of the past. He's prepared to fill your days with reasons to give Him praise.

Joni Eareckson Tada

God specializes in taking tragedy and turning it into triumph. The greater the tragedy, the greater the potential for triumph.

Charles Stanley

He is the God of wholeness and restoration.

Stormie Omartian

QUESTIONS TO CONSIDER

Do I believe that God can make all things new—including me?

_____

_____

Do I take time each day to be still and let God give me perspective and direction?

_____

_____

Am I getting enough rest, and am I spending enough time with God?

_____

_____

A PRAYER FOR TODAY

Dear Lord, You have the power to make all things new. Renew my strength, Father, and renew my hope for the future. Today and every day, Lord, let me draw comfort and courage from Your promises and from Your unending love. Amen

Day 27

A New Sense of Purpose

You will show me the way of life, granting me the joy of your presence and the pleasures of living with you forever.

Psalm 16:11 NLT

The Focus for Today

Their distress is due entirely to their deliberate
determination to use themselves for
a purpose other than God's.

Oswald Chambers

If you're suffering through tough times, you may be asking yourself "What does God want me to do next?" Perhaps you're pondering your future, uncertain of your plans, unsure of your next step. But even if you don't have a clear plan for the next step of your life's journey, you may rest assured that God does.

God has a plan for the universe, and He has a plan for you. He understands that plan as thoroughly and completely as He knows you. If you seek God's will earnestly and prayerfully, He will make His plans known to you in His own time and in His own way.

Do you sincerely want to discover God's purpose for your life? If so, you must first be willing to live in accordance with His commandments. You must also study God's Word and be watchful for His signs. Finally, you should open yourself up to the Creator every day—beginning with this one—and you must have faith that He will soon reveal His plans to you.

Sometimes, God's plans and purposes may seem unmistakably clear to you. If so, push ahead. But other times, He may lead you through the wilderness before He directs you to the Promised Land. So be patient and keep seeking His will for your life. When you do, you'll be amazed at the marvelous things that an all-powerful, all-knowing God can do.

SOMETHING TO REMEMBER

If your life has been turned upside down, you may find yourself searching for something new: a different direction, a new purpose, or a fresh start. As you make your plans, be sure to consult God because even now He is leading you toward a goal that only He can see. Your task is to pray, to listen, and to follow His lead.

MORE FROM GOD'S WORD ABOUT PURPOSE

Whatever you do, do all to the glory of God.

1 Corinthians 10:31 NKJV

You're sons of Light, daughters of Day. We live under wide open skies and know where we stand. So let's not sleepwalk through life . . . .

1 Thessalonians 5:5-6 MSG

We look at this Son and see the God who cannot be seen. We look at this Son and see God's original purpose in everything created.

Colossians 1:15 MSG

We know that all things work together for the good of those who love God: those who are called according to His purpose.

Romans 8:28 HCSB

I will instruct you and show you the way to go; with My eye on you, I will give counsel.

Psalm 32:8 HCSB

MORE POWERFUL IDEAS ABOUT PURPOSE

There is something about having endured great loss that brings purity of purpose and strength of character.

Barbara Johnson

One of the more significant things God will bring out of our grief and depression is an ability to walk constructively with others through theirs. In fact, one of the purposes of God's comfort is to equip us to comfort others.

David B. Biebel

Whatever clouds you face today, ask Jesus, the light of the world, to help you look behind the cloud to see His glory and His plans for you.

Billy Graham

Some things are so important to God that they are worth interrupting the happiness and health of His children in order to accomplish them.

Charles Stanley

The greatest tragedy is not death, but life without purpose.

Rick Warren

QUESTIONS TO CONSIDER

Do I understand the importance of discovering (or rediscovering, if necessary) God's unfolding purpose for my life?

_____

_____

Do I consult God on matters great and small?

_____

_____

Do I pray about my plans for the future, and do I remain open to the opportunities and challenges that God places before me?

_____

_____

A PRAYER FOR TODAY

Dear Lord, let Your purposes be my purposes. Let Your priorities be my priorities. Let Your will be my will. Let Your Word be my guide. And, let me grow in faith and in wisdom today and every day. Amen

Day 28

TIME FOR SERVICE

But he who is greatest among you shall be your servant.
Matthew 23:11 NKJV

THE FOCUS FOR TODAY

God wants us to serve Him with a willing spirit,
one that would choose no other way.
Beth Moore

Grief visits all of us who live long and love deeply. When we lose a loved one, or when we experience any other profound loss, darkness overwhelms us for a while, and it seems as if our purpose for living has vanished. Thankfully, God has other plans.

The Christian faith, as communicated through the words of the Holy Bible, is a healing faith. It offers comfort in times of trouble, courage for our fears, hope instead of hopelessness. For Christians, the grave is not a final resting-place; it is a place of transition. Through the healing words of God's promises, Christians understand that the Lord continues to manifest His plan in good times and bad.

If you are experiencing the intense pain of a recent loss, or if you are still mourning a loss from long ago, perhaps you are now ready to begin the next stage of your journey with God. If so, be mindful of this fact: As a wounded survivor, you will have countless opportunities to serve others. And by serving others, you will bring purpose and meaning to the suffering you've endured.

FIND PURPOSE IN SERVICE

If you genuinely seek to discover God's unfolding purpose for your life, you must ask yourself this question: "How does God want me to serve others?"

Whatever your path, whatever your calling, you may be certain of this: service to others is an integral part of God's plan for your life. Christ was the ultimate servant, the Savior who gave His life for mankind. As His followers, we, too, must become humble servants.

Every single day of your life, including this one, God will give you opportunities to serve Him by serving His children. Welcome those opportunities with open arms. They are God's gift to you, His way of allowing you to achieve greatness in His kingdom.

SOMETHING TO REMEMBER

Wherever you happen to be—whatever your age, whatever your loss—you can find people to help and ways to serve. And the time to begin serving is now.

MORE FROM GOD'S WORD ABOUT SERVING OTHERS

So prepare your minds for service and have self-control.

1 Peter 1:13 NCV

Let this mind be in you which was also in Christ Jesus, who . . . made Himself of no reputation, taking the form of a bondservant, and coming in the likeness of men.

Philippians 2:5,7 NKJV

Therefore, since we receive a kingdom which cannot be shaken, let us show gratitude, by which we may offer to God an acceptable service with reverence and awe . . . .

Hebrews 12:28 NASB

Suppose a brother or a sister is without clothes and daily food. If one of you says to him, "Go, I wish you well; keep warm and well fed," but does nothing about his physical needs, what good is it?

James 2:15-16 NIV

But a Samaritan, as he traveled, came where the man was; and when he saw him, he took pity on him. He went to him and bandaged his wounds, pouring on oil and wine. Then he put the man on his own donkey, took him to an inn and took care of him.

Luke 10:33-34 NIV

MORE POWERFUL IDEAS ABOUT SERVING OTHERS

No life can surpass that of a man who quietly continues to serve God in the place where providence has placed him.

C. H. Spurgeon

Have thy tools ready; God will find thee work.

Charles Kingsley

In the very place where God has put us, whatever its limitations, whatever kind of work it may be, we may indeed serve the Lord Christ.

Elisabeth Elliot

A Christian is a perfectly free lord of all, subject to none. A Christian is a perfectly dutiful servant of all, subject to all.

Martin Luther

You can judge how far you have risen in the scale of life by asking one question: How wisely and how deeply do I care? To be Christianized is to be sensitized. Christians are people who care.

E. Stanley Jones

QUESTIONS TO CONSIDER

Do I believe that I can use my own suffering as a way of helping others?

_____

_____

Do I believe that a willingness to serve others is a sign of greatness in God's eyes?

_____

_____

Do I believe that I am surrounded by opportunities to serve and that I should take advantage of those opportunities?

_____

_____

A PRAYER FOR TODAY
Dear Lord, I seek to live a meaningful life; I will turn to You to find that meaning. I will study Your Word, I will obey Your commandments, I will trust Your providence, and I will honor Your Son. Give me Your blessings, Father, and lead me along a path that is pleasing to You, today, tomorrow, and forever. Amen

Day 29

JUMP-STARTING YOUR LIFE

Therefore, get your minds ready for action,
being self-disciplined, and set your hope completely
on the grace to be brought to you
at the revelation of Jesus Christ.
1 Peter 1:13 HCSB

THE FOCUS FOR TODAY

Let us not be content to wait and see what will happen,
but give us the determination to make
the right things happen.
Peter Marshall

Once the fog of grief begins to lift, it's time to reengage with the world. The willingness to take action—even if the outcome of that action is uncertain—is an effective way to combat hopelessness. When you decide to roll up your sleeves and begin tackling the challenges that confront you, you'll feel empowered.

The advice of American publisher Cyrus Curtis still rings true: "Believe in the Lord and he will do half the work—the last half."

So, today and every day, ask God for these things: clear perspective, mountain-moving faith, and the courage to do what needs doing. After all, no problem is too big for God—not even yours.

LOOK TO THE FUTURE

Because we are saved by a risen Christ, we can have hope for the future, no matter how troublesome our present circumstances may seem. After all, God has promised that we are His throughout eternity. And, He has told us that we must place our hopes in Him.

Of course, we will face disappointments and heartbreaks while we are here on earth, but these are only temporary defeats. Of course, this world can be a place of trials and tribulations, but when we place our trust in the Giver of all things good, we are secure. God has promised us peace, joy, and eternal life. And God keeps His promises today, tomorrow, and forever.

Are you willing to place your future in the hands of a loving and all-knowing God? Do you trust in the ultimate goodness of His plan for your life? Will you face today's challenges with optimism and hope? You should. After all, God created you for a very important purpose: His purpose. And you still have important work to do: His work.

Today, as you live in the present and look to the future, remember that God has a plan for you. Act—and believe—accordingly.

SOMETHING TO REMEMBER

You can use your own suffering as a way to help others . . . and at the appropriate time that's precisely what you should do. (Galatians 6:2)

MORE FROM GOD'S WORD ABOUT GETTING BUSY

Are there those among you who are truly wise and understanding? Then they should show it by living right and doing good things with a gentleness that comes from wisdom.

James 3:13 NCV

Do what God's teaching says; when you only listen and do nothing, you are fooling yourselves.

James 1:22 NCV

For the Kingdom of God is not just fancy talk; it is living by God's power.

1 Corinthians 4:20 NLT

But one thing I do: Forgetting what is behind and straining toward what is ahead, I press on toward the goal to win the prize for which God has called me heavenward in Christ Jesus.

Philippians 3:13-14 NIV

Be strong and brave, and do the work. Don't be afraid or discouraged, because the Lord God, my God, is with you. He will not fail you or leave you.

1 Chronicles 28:20 NCV

MORE POWERFUL IDEAS ABOUT GETTING BUSY

In times of deepest suffering it is the faithful carrying out of ordinary duties that brings the greatest consolation.

Elisabeth Elliot

I must lose myself in action lest I wither in despair.

Alfred, Lord Tennyson

The cure for grief is motion.

Elbert Hubbard

Paul did one thing. Most of us dabble in forty things. Are you a doer or a dabbler?

Vance Havner

Every time you refuse to face up to life and its problems, you weaken your character.

E. Stanley Jones

Take courage.
We walk in the
wilderness today and in
the Promised Land
tomorrow.

—

D. L. Moody

MORE POWERFUL IDEAS ABOUT THE FUTURE

You can look forward with hope, because one day there will be no more separation, no more scars, and no more suffering in My Father's House. It's the home of your dreams!

Anne Graham Lotz

Allow your dreams a place in your prayers and plans. God-given dreams can help you move into the future He is preparing for you.

Barbara Johnson

The Christian believes in a fabulous future.

Billy Graham

Every experience God gives us, every person he brings into our lives, is the perfect preparation for the future that only he can see.

Corrie ten Boom

Joy comes from knowing God loves me and knows who I am and where I'm going . . . that my future is secure as I rest in Him.

James Dobson

QUESTIONS TO CONSIDER

Do I believe that God still has important work for me to do?

_____

_____

Am I willing to do the difficult work of jump-starting my life?

_____

_____

Am I praying for God's guidance and God's peace?

_____

_____

A PRAYER FOR TODAY

_Dear Lord, I have heard Your Word, and I have felt
Your presence in my heart; let me act accordingly. Let
my words and deeds serve as a testimony to the changes
You have made in my life. Let me praise You, Father,
by following in the footsteps of Your Son, and let others
see Him through me. Amen_

Day 30

FOLLOW HIM

Then Jesus said to His disciples, "If anyone wants to come with Me, he must deny himself, take up his cross, and follow Me. For whoever wants to save his life will lose it, but whoever loses his life because of Me will find it."
Matthew 16:24-25 HCSB

THE FOCUS FOR TODAY

You who suffer take heart.
Christ is the answer to sorrow.

Billy Graham

As you move through and beyond your time of grief, you must walk with Jesus every day. Jesus loved you so much that He endured unspeakable humiliation and suffering for you. How will you respond to Christ's sacrifice? Will you take up His cross and follow Him—during good times and hard times—or will you choose another path? When you place your hopes squarely at the foot of the cross, when you place Jesus squarely at the center of your life, you will be transformed.

Do you seek to fulfill God's purpose for your life? Do you seek spiritual abundance? Would you like to partake in "the peace that passes all understanding"? Then follow Christ. Follow Him by picking up His cross today, tomorrow, and every day of your life. When you do, you will quickly discover that Christ's love has the power to change everything, including you.

YOUR ETERNAL JOURNEY

Eternal life is not an event that begins when you die. Eternal life begins when you invite Jesus into your heart right here on earth. So it's important to remember that God's plans for you are not limited to the ups and downs of everyday life. If you've allowed Jesus to reign over your heart, you've already begun your eternal journey.

Today, give praise to the Creator for His priceless gift, the gift of eternal life. And then, when you've offered Him your thanks and your praise, share His Good News with all who cross your path.

SOMETHING TO REMEMBER

Think about your relationship with Jesus: what it is, and what it can be. Then, as you embark upon the next phase of your life's journey, be sure to walk with your Savior every step of the way.

MORE FROM GOD'S WORD ABOUT
FOLLOWING CHRIST

For God so loved the world, that he gave his only begotten Son, that whosoever believeth in him should not perish, but have everlasting life.

John 3:16 KJV

And this is the testimony: that God has given us eternal life, and this life is in His Son. He who has the Son has life; he who does not have the Son of God does not have life.

1 John 5:11-12 NKJV

These things I have written to you who believe in the name of the Son of God, that you may know that you have eternal life.

1 John 5:13 NKJV

Don't be troubled. You trust God, now trust in me. There are many rooms in my Father's home, and I am going to prepare a place for you. If this were not so, I would tell you plainly. When everything is ready, I will come and get you, so that you will always be with me where I am.

John 14:1-3 NLT

MORE FROM GOD'S WORD ABOUT ETERNAL LIFE

We do not want you to be uninformed, brothers, concerning those who are asleep, so that you will not grieve like the rest, who have no hope. Since we believe that Jesus died and rose again, in the same way God will bring with Him those who have fallen asleep through Jesus.

1 Thessalonians 4:13-14 HCSB

Jesus said to her, "I am the resurrection and the life. The one who believes in Me, even if he dies, will live. Everyone who lives and believes in Me will never die—ever. Do you believe this?"

John 11:25-26 HCSB

Pursue righteousness, godliness, faith, love, endurance, and gentleness. Fight the good fight for the faith; take hold of eternal life, to which you were called and have made a good confession before many witnesses.

1 Timothy 6:11-12 HCSB

MORE POWERFUL IDEAS ABOUT FOLLOWING CHRIST

The deepest moments of spiritual fellowship with the living Christ are the direct result of intense suffering.

John MacArthur

It is true of every stinging experience of our lives: Jesus, and Jesus alone, can rescue us.

Franklin Graham

When you read the four Gospels, you discover a remarkable thing: Jesus didn't explain suffering, but rather experienced it and did all He could to relieve it.

Warren Wiersbe

No matter what trials we face, Christ never leaves us.

Billy Graham

Your choice to either receive or reject the Lord Jesus Christ will determine where you spend eternity.

Anne Graham Lotz

If you are a believer, your judgment will not determine your eternal destiny. Christ's finished work on Calvary was applied to you the moment you accepted Christ as Savior.

Beth Moore

MORE POWERFUL IDEAS ABOUT ETERNAL LIFE

Our pain is with us for a little while. Our God is with us forever.

Marie T. Freeman

The believing Christian has hope as he stands at the grave of a loved one who is with the Lord, for he knows that the separation is not forever. It is a glorious truth that those who are in Christ never see each other for the last time.

Billy Graham

He who has no vision of eternity will never get a true hold of time.

Thomas Carlyle

We'll spend eternity exploring and rejoicing in the unsearchable riches of God's character, purpose, love, Living Word, and astounding creativity.

Susan Lenzkes

Live near to God, and all things will appear little to you in comparison with eternal realities.

Robert Murray McCheyne

QUESTIONS TO CONSIDER

Am I attempting to follow in Christ's footsteps, despite my pain?

_____

_____

Do I really believe that my relationship with Jesus should be one of servant and Master? And am I behaving like His servant?

_____

_____

Do I believe that in time I will experience the spiritual abundance that the Bible describes in John 10:10?

_____

_____

A PRAYER FOR TODAY

Dear Jesus, because I am Your disciple, I will trust You, I will obey Your teachings, and I will share Your Good News. You have given me life abundant and life eternal, and I will follow You today and forever. Amen